A Bible Study for Individuals or Small Groups

The Despicable Dozen

Bad Guys of the Bible

Timothy J. Mulder

despicable adjective

de•spi•ca•ble

: deserving to be despised; so worthless or obnoxious as to rouse moral indignation

: very unpleasant or bad, causing strong feelings of dislike:

- *despicable* behavior
- He's a *despicable* human being!
- It was *despicable* of her to lie about her friend.

A Plea to Repent

While we can never know for sure where someone else will go when they die, most of these individuals showed no evidence of a relationship with God that would indicate salvation. Many of them had an opportunity for repentance but failed to take it. Indeed, several were confronted with their sins and given time by God to turn from them. Some were even exhorted to do so by others or even God Himself. And yet they clung to their sins or their pride and stubbornly refused and rejected God. Don't be like them! Don't let your sins take you to Hell!

Don't be like Delilah and pursue worthless idols of fame and money and pass from existence empty and alone. Don't live in a pattern of excuse making so you are blind to your sins and, like King Saul, be forever removed from God's favor. Don't be like King Herod, so wrapped up in anxiety and fear that you live in fight or flight mode, lashing out against others in a never-ending search for security that can only be found in God. Don't let your children be victims in your pursuit of sin like Herod Antipas and Herodias. Don't be like Achan and refuse to unearth the sins hoarded in your tent for a tomorrow that will never come.

But take heart! We have a Savior whose death purchased our freedom from these sins with His blood and freely offers us the gift of restoration to the Father and eternal life. If you cannot say with confidence that you will be with Him in Heaven, ask Him now to save you! The Holy Spirit will enter your heart and you will know peace like you have never known.

If you are a believer but have forgotten your first love or have let the noise of the world crowd the love of God from your heart, let this book be a guide to root out these common sins from your life, God will do what it takes to get your attention, even if He has to turn you into a cow. Repent and be forgiven today!

In His Grace,

Tim and Michelle Mulder

Table of Contents

I

Introduction

―――――◦⚬◦―――――

2 TIMOTHY 3:16-17

"All Scripture is breathed out by God and profitable for teaching,
for reproof, for correction, and for training in righteousness,
that the man of God may be complete, equipped for every good work."

―――――◦⚬◦―――――

BROWSE THE BIBLE STUDY SECTION at any Christian bookseller or website, and you will see plenty of Bible studies on the heroes of the faith:

Moses, David, Deborah, Paul, and so on. Without a doubt, God used these great men and women of the faith to accomplish His will. We would do well to study them. But what makes a character a hero? Something I love about Scripture is how beautifully flawed the people are. Modern royalty and celebrity scandals have nothing on the dysfunctional family dynamics portrayed in God's Word. With such morally grey people, how do we decide whose good outweighed their bad, or vice versa?

King David, for example, was the greatest king of Israel and the author of many of the Psalms. Scripture repeatedly calls him, "a man after God's own heart."[1] Being a man after God's own heart means living your life in harmony with the Lord. What is important to God is important to you. What angers Him angers you. When God says to turn right, you turn right. You want your life to reflect God's heart.

But didn't King David sin with Bathsheba and have her husband Uriah killed? How could God still call David a man after His own heart when David committed such terrible sins? Was he still a man after God's own heart?

The mighty often fall hard, and David's fall included adultery, lying, murder, and the resulting death of his son. As we will see, these terrible deeds could have earned him a place in The Despicable Dozen. Should he be on our list? Why is he not considered evil? The difference between David and the characters classically considered the villains of Scripture is centered on what happened *after* he sinned. David repented. Repentance requires confession of sin, turning away from sin and turning toward God. David confessed his sin in 2 Samuel 12:13, "David said to Nathan, 'I have sinned against the LORD.' Then Nathan replied, "The LORD also has put away your sin; you shall not die.'" Admitting his sin and asking for forgiveness (confession) was half of the equation. The other half of repentance is reconciliation, which is turning from sin and toward God.

---

[1] 1 Samuel 13:14, "But now your kingdom shall not continue. The LORD has sought out a man *after His own heart*, and the LORD has commanded him to be prince over his people, because you have not kept what the LORD commanded you." (Italics added.)

Psalm 51 records David's heartfelt sorrow over his sin and longing to be restored to God:

> Have mercy on me, O God, according to your steadfast love; according to your abundant mercy blot out my transgressions. Wash me thoroughly from my iniquity and cleanse me from my sin!
>
> (Psalm 51:1-2)

The Psalm continues reflecting David's genuine desire for true reconciliation with God. This is what made David a man after God's own heart. Like all imperfect humans, he failed at times. What set David apart was that he earnestly sought and experienced forgiveness and restoration of communion with God. Ultimately, David loved God's law and sought to follow it. As a man after God's own heart, David serves as a role model for all of us. It is right that we should study his life and words and seek to emulate his repentance.

What about the terrible, evil people in the Scriptures? Why are there no Bible studies written about them? No hero story is complete without an anti-hero, villain, or antagonist. God's inerrant word includes these villains for a reason. Are they *only* included to oppose the hero and make them look good? By no means! Studying them will allow us to better understand God's sovereignty: He uses the good guys and the bad guys of Scripture to accomplish His perfect will. This study will look at the baddest of the bad: the twelve most evil villains in the Bible, The Despicable Dozen. (This list is not all-inclusive, as there is no shortage of evil people in Scripture.) As a key difference between most of these characters and King David hinges on the issue of repentance, we will also consider whether or not the character displayed repentance, true or otherwise.

Is God the Author of Evil?

Just as we needed to establish repentance as a key difference between people considered heroes or villains in the Bible, we also need to answer a critical question about God's relationship with evil. It is common for people to ask how a loving God can allow suffering and evil in the world. How can a sovereign God let bad things happen? God is sovereign over both good *and* evil. However, in today's culture, we don't like to think of it that way. We tend to credit God with the good in the world, but not the evil. Though God is *sovereign over evil*, we must be careful not to say that He is the *cause of evil*. Proverbs 15:3 says, "The eyes of the LORD are in every place, keeping watch on the evil and the good."

To better answer questions such as "How did evil get here?" and "Did God create evil?" we must understand God's attributes. Attributes are used to describe a quality or characteristic of someone that help us better understand them. If you were to use attributes to describe a friend, you might use words like kind, funny or loyal. Scripture describes God by using His many attributes: He is holy, sovereign, eternal, loving, omnipotent (all-powerful), and omniscient (all-knowing), to name a few. The word holy means "set apart." God is set apart from everything sinful. When we say that God is holy, we are saying that His character has no trace of sin or evil.[2]

We know that holy God created the universe in six days, and initially, there was no sin. Everything God made was "good" or "very good."[3] So where did evil come from? Sin entered the world due to man's rebellion against God, not because God created sin. Man bears complete

---

[2] There are many verses about God's holiness. Here are just a few: Isaiah 6:3b - "Holy, holy, holy is the LORD of hosts; the whole earth is full of his glory!" Revelation 4:8, "And the four living creatures, each of them with six wings, are full of eyes all around and within, and day and night they never cease to say, 'Holy, holy, holy, is the LORD God Almighty, who was and is and is to come!'" Psalm 77:13 – "Your way, O God, is holy. What god is great like our God?" 1 Peter 1:16 – "Since it is written, 'You shall be holy, for I am holy.'"
[3] Genesis 1:31, "And God saw everything that He had made, and behold, it was *very good.* And there was evening and there was morning, the sixth day." (Italics added.)

responsibility for sin. As such, *all evil in the universe comes from the sin of fallen man.* Scripture affirms that God is not the author of evil.[4]

God is not the author of evil, but He is sovereign[5] over it. Evil did *not* take God by surprise. It is *not* an interruption of His eternal plan. It did *not* cause God to stop and come up with plan B. God has already written the end of the story and has worked *all* of the events of Scripture to accomplish it. Isaiah 46:9-10, tells us, "Remember the former things of old; for I am God, and there is no other; I am God, and there is none like me, *declaring the end from the beginning* and from ancient times things not yet done, saying, 'My counsel shall stand, and I *will accomplish all my purpose.*'" (Italics added.) In other words, God wrote the end of humanity's story taking evil into account. He uses the good and the bad to accomplish His purpose. His sovereign will cannot be thwarted.

Without Further Ado… Who Made the List?
Before we look at this Biblical rogue's gallery, let's discuss qualifications for inclusion into our hall of shame. The twelve selected for this study include individuals guilty of heinous sins, but others are included because of *whom* they sinned against. Our study will examine liars, adulterers, traitors, murderers, corrupt politicians, human traffickers, and despots guilty of murder and infanticide on an unfathomable scale.

This study will examine these evildoers in order of appearance in the Bible, not in order of a scale of badness.[6] The intent is not to point fingers at Biblical villains and their sins but to show how God has used each of them to accomplish His perfect, sovereign will. Upon finishing this study,

---

[4] Here are a few verses that speak of God not being the author of evil: James 1:13 – "Let no one say when he is tempted, 'I am being tempted by God,' for God cannot be tempted with evil, and He Himself tempts no one." 1 John 1:5 – "This is the message we have heard from Him and proclaim to you, that God is light, and in Him is no darkness at all." Genesis 1:31 – "And God saw everything that He had made, and behold, it was very good."
[5] Sovereignty is the doctrine that maintains that God has the power, authority, and right to rule over creation.
[6] It is surprisingly difficult to determine a "scale of badness" for these villains. It is subjective and highly dependent upon the reader's opinion - but does make for lively and interesting discussions!

you should have a much better understanding of the sovereignty of God and His ability to use both good and evil to accomplish His eternal plan.

People complain that the Bible is full of stories and is not relevant to our culture. However, you may be surprised to find that the temptations and pressures faced by these individuals are familiar to our lives today. In fact, if we examine our hearts, we are more like these villains than we are the heroes of the faith.

Shakespeare once said that people "commit the oldest sins in the newest kind of ways."[7] What he meant is that, even though society may change and technologies advance our way of living, our sin natures remain the same. "It highlights the inherent human tendency to engage in unethical behavior and adapt to changing times while perpetuating these timeless vices."[8] In this instance, the Bible agrees with Mr. Shakespeare. In Ecclesiastes 1:9, we are told, "What has been is what will be, and what has been done is what will be done, and there is nothing new under the sun." In that way, these stories serve as cautionary tales of how sin can entrap us and drag us to destruction.

The remainder of this introduction is an overview of the bad guys that made the list:

1. Cain – his jealousy and rage led him to become the world's first murderer. Cain single-handedly killed twenty-five percent of the earth's population in one day!

2. Joseph's brothers – a unique example of a mob mentality leading to assault, human trafficking, fraud, theft, and lying to their grieving father for years.

3. Pharaoh – mandated state sponsored infanticide to secure his place on the throne, claiming that the Hebrews presented a threat to national security.

---

[7] William Shakespeare, *Henry IV*, Act 4, Scene 4.
[8] https://quotation.io/quote/commit-oldest-sins-newest-kind-ways Accessed September 9, 2024.

4. Achan – his greed and disobedience to God resulted in the deaths of 36 innocent men and the executions of his wife, sons, and daughters.

5. Delilah – a treacherous femme-fatale whose betrayal of Samson has made her infamous and her name synonymous with deceit.

6. King Saul – his disobedience and arrogant self-righteousness led God to remove His spirit from him and "regret making him king."[9]

7. King Ahab and Queen Jezebel – the most evil and corrupt leaders in the history of Israel.[10] Ahab and Jezebel were guilty of lying, theft, and murder among other crimes.

8. King Nebuchadnezzar – the king of Babylon who ruthlessly annihilated entire nations (including Egypt and Israel,) committed genocide, and enslaved entire populations; yet was not punished for these atrocities, but for the sin of pride in not giving God the credit for his accomplishments.

9. King Herod the Great – king of Judea, abused his position of power to protect and serve himself; lied to the Magi and murdered Bethlehem's little boys in an attempt to kill Jesus.

10. "King" Herod Antipas and Queen Herodias – tetrarchs[11] of Judea under Roman occupation. Their adulterous and incestuous marriage earned them the public condemnation of John the Baptist, whom they wrongfully imprisoned, executed by beheading, and delivered his head on a platter at Antipas' birthday party.

11. Pontius Pilate – the governor of Judea. His cowardly acquiescence to mob rule led to Jesus' conviction and crucifixion.

---

[9] 1 Samuel 15:10-11, "The word of the LORD came to Samuel: [11] 'I regret that I have made Saul king, for he has turned back from following me and has not performed my commandments.' And Samuel was angry, and he cried to the LORD all night."

[10] 1 Kings 16:30, "And Ahab the son of Omri did evil in the sight of the LORD, more than all who were before him."

[11] A tetrarch was one of the sons of Herod the Great who ruled over a portion of his kingdom but was not considered a king. Herod Antipas liked to call himself a king.

12. Judas Iscariot – his betrayal of Jesus to the Sanhedrin after spending three years as one of Jesus' closest companions has made his name synonymous with betrayal and treason.

I hope that as you go through *The Despicable Dozen,* you will come to understand God's sovereignty over evil and how He uses *all* things to accomplish His will. And that you will see how these real examples of some of the worst sins in the Bible were motivated by pressures and temptations that plague us still.

My other goal in this study is that you will see the sins of these people and how they continue to be acted out in our own lives and use that knowledge to dig up the floor of the tent of your heart. If you didn't understand that analogy, wait until you read the chapter on Achan.

Additionally, if you feel that a Bible character was not included in the Despicable Dozen that should have been, please email me at timothyjmulder@gmail.com. I'd love to hear what you think!

Cain Smiting Abel with God's Expulsion of Cain from the Garden of Eden,
Marco and Sebastian Ricci. Painting: oil on canvas, 17th century.

1

Cain

GENESIS 4:1-17

Now Adam knew Eve his wife, and she conceived and bore Cain, saying, "I have gotten a man with the help of the LORD." [2] And again, she bore his brother Abel. Now Abel was a keeper of sheep, and Cain a worker of the ground. [3] In the course of time Cain brought to the LORD an offering of the fruit of the ground, [4] and Abel also brought of the firstborn of his flock and of their fat portions. And the LORD had regard[1] for Abel and his offering, [5] but for Cain and his offering he had no regard[1]. So, Cain was very angry, and his face fell. [6] The LORD said to Cain, "Why are you angry,

---

[1] The Hebrew word translated "had regard" can also mean "viewed favorably."

and why has your face fallen? ⁷ If you do well, will you not be accepted? And if you do not do well, sin is crouching at the door. Its desire is contrary to you, but you must rule over it."

⁸ Cain spoke to Abel his brother. And when they were in the field, Cain rose up against his brother Abel and killed him. ⁹ Then the LORD said to Cain, "Where is Abel your brother?" He said "I do not know; am I my brother's keeper?" ¹⁰ And the LORD said, "What have you done? The voice of your brother's blood is crying to me from the ground. ¹¹ And now you are cursed from the ground, which has opened its mouth to receive your brother's blood from your hand. ¹² When you work the ground, it shall no longer yield to you its strength. You shall be a fugitive and a wanderer on the earth." ¹³ Cain said to the LORD, "My punishment is greater than I can bear. ¹⁴ Behold, you have driven me today away from the ground, and from your face I shall be hidden. I shall be a fugitive and a wanderer on the earth, and whoever finds me will kill me." ¹⁵ Then the LORD said to him, "Not so! If anyone kills Cain, vengeance shall be taken on him sevenfold." And the LORD put a mark on Cain, lest any who found him should attack him. ¹⁶ Then Cain went away from the presence of the LORD and settled in the land of Nod, east of Eden. ¹⁷ Cain knew his wife, and she conceived and bore Enoch. When he built a city, he called the name of the city after the name of his son, Enoch.

CAIN, THE ELDEST SON OF Adam and Eve, has an important place in human history. He was the first human to be conceived and born. He also committed the first murder in history, his younger brother Abel. In doing so, Cain killed one quarter of the world's population! No one else even comes close! Cain followed in his parents' footsteps by sinning and being punished for his sin.

Not only did God promise offspring to Adam and Eve, but He promised offspring that would crush the serpent's head. Cain, in Hebrew means "acquired." As we will see in Genesis 4:1[2], after Cain was born, Eve said that she had gotten (or acquired or received) "a man with the help of the LORD." Abel's name provides us with a bit of foreshadowing. Abel's name in Hebrew means "breath" or "vapor."[3] It shows that Abel, in comparison to others, would be on earth only for a short time.

Adam had an important relationship with the ground in the Garden of Eden.[4] Adam's primary responsibility was to tend the garden and oversee the animals therein. Cain followed in the footsteps of his father and, according to Genesis 4:2[5] "worked the ground." When Adam sinned, his punishment was difficulty in cultivating the ground. When Cain sinned, his punishment was worse than Adam's: Cain was driven from the ground. According to verse 12,[6] the ground would no longer yield crops to Cain. Cain would no longer harvest fruits and vegetables from the ground. He would live the balance of his life as a gatherer, forever looking for his food.

The Offerings of Cain and Abel

A fundamental assumption in verses 1-7 is that man is to worship God. God is to be worshipped by a sacrifice in accordance with the faith of those worshiping Him. In verses 3 and 4, both brothers brought offerings *to the LORD*. This implies that they knew where God met with man and brought their offerings to Him. Both brothers understood there to be a specific

---

[2] Genesis 4:1, "Now Adam knew Eve, his wife, and she conceived and bore Cain, saying, 'I have gotten a man with the help of the LORD.'"
[3] The Hebrew root word for Abel's name is *hevel*, which means "breath" or "vapor." It is the same word used in Ecclesiates 1:2, "Vanity of vanities, says the Preacher, vanity of vanities! All is vanity" and Ecclesiastes 12:8, "Vanity of vanities, says the Preacher; all is vanity."
[4] The Hebrew word for land is *Adama*, which is the root word of Adam's name.
[5] Genesis 4:2, "Now Abel was a keeper of sheep, and Cain a *worker of the ground*." (Italics added.)
[6] Genesis 4:12, "When you work the ground, it shall no longer yield to you its strength. You shall be a fugitive and a wanderer on the earth."

means of worship. They both knew that God was to be worshipped through sacrifice.

Keep in mind, Cain was not an atheist. He believed in and worshipped God. The difference between Cain and Abel's offerings was their faith. The heart of the issue was their attitude toward God and the nature of their sacrifices. Abel brought the firstborn of his flocks as well as the fat portions. These are the choicest parts of the best of his animals. According to Hebrews 11:4,[7] God accepted Abel's offering.

Cain's actions displayed the condition of his heart. While Abel brought the best that he had, Cain was going through the motions by bringing an offering of the fruit of the ground[8] to the LORD. Verse 3[9] does not say that he brought the first fruits but rather the fruit of the ground. This may imply fruit that has fallen to the ground, suggesting damage or rot. One can imagine Cain picking up the bruised, overripe, worm-ridden fruit or gathering the scattered grains from the dirt of his fields to offer to his God.[10]

Why did God not accept Cain's offering? Cain's offering was bloodless. Hebrews 9:22[11] says, "Without the shedding of blood, there is no forgiveness of sins." This is one reason God rejected Cain's offering. Cain's offering did not point to Jesus' blood atonement. Cain did the minimum of what God required. Rather than give with joy, he gave with a sullen attitude. Certainly, the sub-par items he chose for his sacrifice

---

[7] Hebrews 11:4, "By faith Abel offered to God a more acceptable sacrifice than Cain, through which he was commended as righteous, God commending him by accepting his gifts. And through his faith, though he died, he still speaks."
[8] Genesis 4:5, "But for Cain and his offering he had no regard. So, Cain was very angry, and his face fell."
[9] Genesis 4:3, "In the course of time Cain brought to the LORD an offering of the fruit of the ground."
[10] Have you ever told a child, "Don't eat that!" after they drop a tasty morsel of food in the dirt. (The three second rule not-withstanding.) You would never let your child eat contaminated food from the ground. Cain, however, picked it up, brushed it off, and brought it to God.
[11] Hebrews 9:22, "Indeed, under the law almost everything is purified with blood, and *without the shedding of blood there is no forgiveness of* sins." (Italics added.)

reflected the attitude with which Cain brought the "fruit of the ground" to the LORD. In addition to the fruits of the ground signifying the dirty, rotten leftovers, or the sweepings from the threshing floor, according to Genesis 3:17,[12] "cursed is the ground." Cain brought as an offering the fruit of what the LORD cursed.

When God rejected Cain's offering, Cain became angry and his face fell. Cain's attitude toward worship was full of pride and self-worship. It was not a matter of whether or not he would worship, but whom he would worship. His anger indicated a heart that was not right with God. He was angry because he couldn't worship God on his own terms. His sin began in the heart and ultimately ended with an outward act of aggression. Cain's actions perfectly follow the path from temptation to sin described in James 1:14-15, "but each person is tempted when he is lured and enticed by his own desire. Then desire when it has conceived gives birth to sin, and sin when it is fully grown brings forth death."

However, God's response to Cain was that of a loving, caring Father. He confronted Cain's anger immediately and encouraged him to do what was right. He sincerely appealed to Cain to do well, repent, and turn back to Him. He explained to Cain that if he did well, he too would be accepted. However, if Cain continued to do wrong, sin would hound him.

Cain had a choice to make - follow the ways of God or follow the ways of sin. God loved Cain and wanted what was best for him, so He again entreated Cain to do what was right, saying, "sin desires to have you, but you must rule over it."[13] Only Cain's repentance could result in divine acceptance. The two verbs "desire" and "rule" are also used in Genesis 3:16 in God's punishment of Eve, "I will sharpen the pain of your pregnancy, and in pain you will give birth. And you will *desire* to control your husband, but he will *rule* over you." (NLT, Italics added.) The point

---

[12] Genesis 3:17, "And to Adam he said, 'Because you have listened to the voice of your wife and have eaten of the tree of which I commanded you, 'You shall not eat of it,' cursed is the ground because of you; in pain you shall eat of it all the days of your life.'"

[13] Genesis 4:7 (NIV), "If you do what is right, will you not be accepted? But if you do not do what is right, sin is crouching at your door; it desires to have you, but you must rule over it."

of God's statements to Eve and Cain is the innate human desire to be in control and how that goal, ironically, leads to being dominated by sin. "The issue for Cain is what will dominate him and have control and mastery over him."[14] The end goal of sin is to dominate those that struggle with it. Sin offered Cain chained oppression in contrast to the freedom of acceptance in God's favor.

God provided Cain a way out,[15] but Cain chose his pride and anger instead, so he was led away by his temptation and sin possessed him to kill his brother. Just as Scripture predicts, sin was a lion who pounced to consume,[16] and Abel's blood flowed.

What about you? Are you like Cain, merely going through the motions of worship? Do you simply show up on Sunday mornings? Or have you prepared to come to worship? Do you tithe with joy or do you give begrudgingly? We all struggle with this at one time or another. Pray to God that he will give you a spirit of thankfulness and joy. Soften your heart. Prepare it for the Lord's day. You are communing with God. Give Him the reverence that He is due.

The Slaying of Abel

Genesis states that Cain spoke to Abel, and it is presumed that he persuaded his brother to go to a field away from their parents where he could execute his plan. Today, Cain would be guilty of premeditated murder. There may have been no human witnesses to the crime, but God saw Cain's actions. Man's sins are never hidden from God.

Why did Cain kill his brother? Was it because he hated him? Or was it because he hated God? I would argue for both reasons. Murder is an act

---

[14] John D. Currid, *Genesis* EPSC Volume 1 (Webster: Evangelical Press, 2003), 133.

[15] 1 Corinthians 10:13, "No temptation has overtaken you that is not common to man. God is faithful, and He will not let you be tempted beyond your ability, but with the temptation He will also provide the way of escape, that you may be able to endure it."

[16] 1 Peter 5:8, "Be sober-minded; be watchful. Your adversary the devil prowls around like a roaring lion, seeking someone to devour."

of hatred toward man and God. Murder is a blatant disregard for those created in God's image.

Though Cain was biologically Adam's son, his attitude and actions indicated that he was the offspring of the serpent from Genesis 3:15[17]. Cain's response to God's questioning followed in the path of his father (the father of lies.) His flippant response showed a hardened heart and a contempt for God, "I don't know; am I my brother's keeper?" There was no evidence of a contrite heart.

Interestingly, Genesis 4 refers to Abel as Cain's brother seven times. However, Cain was never referred to as Abel's brother. Not one time. This is because Cain forfeited his brotherhood when he murdered Abel. As a consequence of his sin, he was now brotherless. *Sin brings isolation from others.*

Cain's Curse

Cain could not hide the murder of his brother any more than Adam and Eve could hide from God behind a bush. The LORD saw Cain's sin and consequently meted out swift and immediate justice. In verse 11, God cursed Cain.

Adam and Eve experienced further consequences of their sin, in that they not only lost their son Abel to murder, but they also lost their son, Cain, to exile. God commanded Cain to be a wanderer on the earth. Cain's punishment was exile, just as his parents were exiled from the Garden of Eden for their sin. *Sin results in exile.*

In verse 12, God told Cain that he would be a fugitive and a wanderer for the rest of his days. Cain was denied the comforts of an established home, family, and community. He was also denied his occupation, which had been the means of his unacceptable sacrifice. But most importantly, he was denied fellowship with God through worship. Cain complained that his punishment was too much to bear and that people would kill him on

---

[17] Genesis 3:15, "I will put enmity between you and the woman, and between your offspring and her offspring; He shall bruise your head, and you shall bruise His heel."

sight. Doesn't that make you want to shake him and remind him that his brother was dead? God's condemnation of the despicable murder of his brother failed to prick his hardened conscience of the need to repent. God used Cain's promise of punishment as an opportunity for Cain to repent. And again, Cain did not. Despite this harsh sentence, Cain disobeyed God again, proving that his lamenting was only selfish whining and he had learned nothing.

"Cain knew his wife, and she conceived and bore Enoch. When he built a city, he called the name of the city after the name of his son, Enoch." Cain *built* a city. It sounds as though he was settling down to me. Remember, in verse 12 when God told Cain that he would be a fugitive and a wanderer for the rest of his days? He was not going to wander any longer. He built a city instead. Did he dedicate that city to God? Absolutely not. He named it after his heir, his son, Enoch.[18]

Cain's response to God's judgment showed no repentance whatsoever. He was more concerned about his punishment than the sin that brought it about. This is worldly sorrow as opposed to godly sorrow. Worldly sorrow says, "I'm sorry I got caught." This is self-consumed sorrow. Godly sorrow says, "I'm sorry I have sinned." Godly sorrow aches at the loss of communion with God and fervently seeks to be restored to His favor. Repentance involves confession and turning to God. Sadly, there is no evidence that Cain ever repented of his sin.

Comparing the First Two Sins

We are four chapters into the Bible, and already, there have been two sins: one committed by Adam and Eve, and one by Cain. Let's compare Cain's sin in Genesis 4 with Adam and Eve's sin in Genesis 3. Cain's sin was against his brother. He was jealous of Abel and Abel's relationship with God, but he didn't want to do what was necessary to restore his own relationship with God. Adam and Eve's sin was against God. They had

---

[18] This is an appeal to the glory of man rather than the glory of God. It foreshadows the events surrounding the Tower of Babel, in which man sought to bring himself glory instead of bringing God the glory.

been deceived that, if they sinned, that they would be like God. Both sins ended in death: The result of Adam and Eve's sin brought with it death for all humanity. The result of Cain's sin was the death of his brother. There is no other way to put it: *sin leads to death.*

Both sins were punished by banishment and isolation: Adam and Eve were banished from the Garden of Eden. Cain was banished and isolated from his family and was commanded to be a wanderer for the rest of his life. Since God is holy, He hates sin. He loathes it. He cannot be around it. Therefore, if God dwelt in the Garden of Eden, He would have to banish Adam and Eve because He cannot be near sin. The same was true with Cain. That way the sins of Cain would not be repeated on any future siblings. *Sin leads to isolation from God.*

There is an interesting parallel between Genesis 3:17[19] and 4:11-12[20]. Verses 11-12 mark an extension of the curse imposed upon Cain's parents in Eden and highlights that every unrighteous action further alienates humankind from God and the earth. Adam's punishment for his sin was the cursing of the ground, which resulted in thorns, thistles, and sweat. Cain's punishment added to Adam's punishment. In verse 12, Cain was told, "When you work the ground, it shall no longer yield to you its strength." Cain's curse brought barrenness to the ground and the resulting possibility of famine. It set a precedent that God would use the ground to communicate His displeasure with His people. The Old Testament is full of stories of droughts and famines, often as a consequence of man's disobedience.

---

[19] Genesis 3:17, "And to Adam He said, 'Because you have listened to the voice of your wife and have eaten of the tree of which I commanded you, 'You shall not eat of it,' cursed is the ground because of you; in pain you shall eat of it all the days of your life.'"

[20] Genesis 4:11-12, "And now you are cursed from the ground, which has opened its mouth to receive your brother's blood from your hand. [12] When you work the ground, it shall no longer yield to you its strength. You shall be a fugitive and a wanderer on the earth."

Genesis 4 fulfills the prophecy of the curse in Genesis 3:15.[21] Cain's sin displays the enmity between the seed of the woman and the seed of the serpent. This is the first time in Scripture that the prophecy of this verse will be confirmed. But certainly not the last.

God's Unfailing Love

In Genesis 4:14, Cain expressed his concern that "whoever finds me will kill me." Who was he worried about? Perhaps Adam and Eve would have been so angry with him that they would have done so. Maybe a future sibling of Cain would seek revenge for the murder of Abel. Cain fretted about his future safety, so God promised to protect him

Regardless of Cain's sin and despite his punishment, God still planned to protect him. This is the highlight of the story! Verse 15 outlines God's plan. "Then the LORD said to him, "Not so! If anyone kills Cain, vengeance shall be taken on him sevenfold."[22] And the LORD put a mark on Cain, lest any who found him should attack him. Despite Cain's actions against God and his brother, despite his sullen unrepentant attitude, God showed him grace. And yet, Cain still did not respond to this grace in repentance. God's grace was glaringly evident in His treatment of Cain and yet it made no difference. God loved Cain so much that He was willing to protect him, a murderer.

Like Cain, our actions and sin do not change who God is. Even when He is meting out His righteous justice, He still offers us grace. God desires our repentance and remains faithful when we are not. Even to a murderer. Romans 5:8 tells us that "God shows his love for us in that while we were still sinners, Christ died for us." We do not have to live a perfect life to approach our heavenly Father. We cannot do anything on our own power

---

[21] Genesis 3:15, "I will put enmity between you and the woman, and between your offspring and her offspring; He shall bruise your head, and you shall bruise His heel." This verse is famously known as the *protoevangelium* because it is the first (*proto*) proclamation of the gospel (*euangelion*). God promised to deal a mortal blow to Satan through the offspring of Eve. When God refers to Eve's offspring, He is referring to Jesus Christ, His only Son, who dealt the final blow to Satan when He died on the cross.

[22] Sevenfold signifies a divine judicial order.

to make Him love us any more than He already does. This is good news! If God will protect Cain, the seed of the serpent, a cold-blooded murderer, how much more will He protect us?[23]

According to Hebrews 12:24, the blood of Abel called out for justice. "And to Jesus, the mediator of a new covenant, and to the sprinkled blood. that speaks a better word than the blood of Abel." The voice of Abel's blood was crying out to God from the ground. Abel's blood demanded restitution from the Author of justice. While Abel's blood[24] cried out for justice, Jesus' blood answered that call for justice. In the early chapters of Genesis, we already see God using the despicable actions of Cain to bring about the gospel of Jesus Christ.

---

[23] Saul was called to service and was renamed Paul, despite how his actions exposed countless early Christians to imprisonment and death. God is in the business of redeeming sinners. Acts 9:1-2, "But Saul, still breathing threats and murder against the disciples of the Lord, went to the high priest [2] and asked him for letters to the synagogues at Damascus, so that if he found any belonging to the Way, men or women, he might bring them bound to Jerusalem."

[24] Bible Trivia: Genesis 4:10 is the first mention of blood in the Bible.

REVIEW QUESTIONS

1. Why was Abel's offering acceptable while Cain's was not? Do you think this is due more to his attitude or the nature of his sacrifice?

2. What was God's response to Abel's murder? How did God's instructions to Cain offer the opportunity for repentance?

3. What are the consequences of Cain's sin? What can we learn about sin from Cain's sin against his brother?

4. Describe similarities between Cain's punishment and Adam and Eve's punishment. How was Cain's punishment an extension of Adam's punishment?

5. The end goal of sin is to dominate those that struggle with it. Have you seen this in your own life or in the lives of others? Can you give some examples?

6. God showed Cain mercy when he sinned. How does God show us mercy when we sin?

7. Cain is not the only murderer to have his life spared. Name other murderers in Scripture who had their lives spared. Were they repentant of their sins?

8. Do you find yourself only going through the motions of worship? Do you approach worship with joy? Or is it just something you do? What does true worship look like?

Joseph and His Brethren, Bartolomé Esteban Murillo. Painting: oil on canvas, 17th century. London: Great Gallery.

2

Joseph's Brothers

GENESIS 37:18-36

They saw him from afar, and before he came near to them, they conspired against him to kill him. ¹⁹ They said to one another, "Here comes this dreamer. ²⁰ Come now, let us kill him and throw him into one of the pits. Then we will say that a fierce animal has devoured him, and we will see what will become of his dreams." ²¹ But when Reuben heard it, he rescued him out of their hands, saying, "Let us not take his life." ²² And Reuben said to them, "Shed no blood; throw him into this pit here in the wilderness, but do not lay a hand on him"—that he might rescue him out of their hand to restore him to his father. ²³ So when Joseph came to his brothers, they stripped him of his robe, the robe of many colors that he *wore.* ^{24} *And they took him and threw him into a pit. The pit was empty; there was no water in it.*

^{25} *Then they sat down to eat. And looking up they saw a caravan of Ishmaelites coming from Gilead, with their camels bearing gum, balm, and myrrh, on their way to carry it down to Egypt.* ^{26} *Then Judah said to his brothers, "What profit is it if we kill our brother and conceal his blood?* ^{27} *Come, let us sell him to the Ishmaelites, and let not our hand be upon him, for he is our brother, our own flesh." And his brothers listened to him.* ^{28} *Then Midianite traders passed by. And they drew Joseph up and lifted him out of the pit and sold him to the Ishmaelites for twenty shekels of silver. They took Joseph to Egypt.*

^{29} *When Reuben returned to the pit and saw that Joseph was not in the pit, he tore his clothes* ^{30} *and returned to his brothers and said, "The boy is gone, and I, where shall I go?"* ^{31} *Then they took Joseph's robe and slaughtered a goat and dipped the robe in the blood.* ^{32} *And they sent the robe of many colors and brought it to their father and said, "This we have found; please identify whether it is your son's robe or not."* ^{33} *And he identified it and said, "It is my son's robe. A fierce animal has devoured him. Joseph is without doubt torn to pieces."* ^{34} *Then Jacob tore his garments and put sackcloth on his loins and mourned for his son many days.* ^{35} *All his sons and all his daughters rose up to comfort him, but he refused to be comforted and said, "No, I shall go down to Sheol to my son, mourning." Thus, his father wept for him.* ^{36} *Meanwhile the Midianites had sold him in Egypt to Potiphar, an officer of Pharaoh, the captain of the guard.*

SHOULD JOSEPH'S BROTHERS APPEAR ON our list of Biblical bad guys? Surely, they were not as bad as Cain. He *killed* his brother. The sons of Israel didn't kill anyone, at least *not this time.*[1] As much as they wanted to kill Joseph, they decided to sell him into slavery instead. However, what they put their father through was reprehensible. After they sold Joseph to the Midianite traders, they told their father, Jacob, that Joseph had been killed. The brothers were batterers, liars, and human traffickers, but from Jacob's perspective, they may as well have been murderers. They stole Joseph from their father and murdered him in their father's heart. Jacob grieved for years over the loss of his favorite son. *And they never told him the truth!*

One of my friends lost his oldest son. He told me he thought things would have gotten easier with time, but years later, he still breaks down and cries several times each week. We instinctively know that burying a child goes against the natural order of things. We are not supposed to bury our kids. We're just not.

Upon reading the rest of the book of Genesis, we know that God was using these events to bring about His will. The way that God does so is known as providence, how God takes care of His people.[2] God works through circumstances and situations – this is how He interacts with His creation. Since this is how God operates, we can trust His providential hand in our relationships, careers, ministries, marriages, parenting, and every other area of our lives.[3]

In time, Joseph will come to see the despicable acts of his brothers through the forgiving lens of God's providence. His later statement of faith

---

[1] Like career offenders, Joseph's brothers did some pretty underhanded things to their enemies, including wiping out an entire city. For example, check out Genesis 34 for details on the infamous "Shechem incident." It is worth the read.

[2] The Westminster Confession of Faith 5.1, "God, who created everything, also upholds everything. He directs, regulates, and governs every creature, action, and thing, from the greatest to the least, by His divine providence. He does so according to His infallible foreknowledge and the voluntary, unchangeable purpose of His will, all to praise the glory of His wisdom, power, justice, goodness, and mercy."

[3] Sarah Ivill, *Judges and Ruth: There is a Redeemer* (Phillipsburg: P&R, 2014), 265.

in God's providence is one of the most beautiful testimonies in Scripture. Genesis 50:20 reads, "As for you, you meant evil against me, but God meant it for good, to bring it about that many people should be kept alive, as they are today."

The Brothers' Hatred for Joseph

Joseph's brothers clearly hated him. Twice in Scripture, we are given insight into their hatred. First, Joseph was their father's favorite son. Joseph was the oldest son of Rachel, Jacob's beloved wife. Nowhere in Scripture does it say Jacob hid the fact that he loved Rachel more than his other wives. Additionally, Joseph was born when Jacob was older, arriving after many years of infertility for Rachel. Since he loved Joseph so much, Jacob presented Joseph with a "robe of many colors."[4] Typically, a coat like this would have reached to the wrists and ankles, such as noblemen and royalty wore.[5] This also would have made it very expensive as dyes were worth far more than gold.[6]

The second reason that Joseph's brothers hated him was because of his dreams in which they bowed down to him. It was bad enough that he had these dreams, but for some reason, Joseph felt it necessary to share those dreams with his brothers and father. In his first dream, Joseph and his brothers were all sheaves of grain. While Joseph's sheaf rose up, the brothers' sheaves of grain bowed down to Joseph's sheaf.[7] In the second

---

[4] Genesis 37:3, "Now Israel (Jacob) loved Joseph more than any other of his sons, because he was the son of his old age. And he made him a robe of many colors."

[5] C.F. Keil, and F. Delitzsch, *The Pentateuch* (Grand Rapids: Eerdmans, 1973), 335.

[6] As an example, Tyrian purple dye was made by the Phoenicians from the secretions of a sea snail called a Murex. It took thousands of these snails to produce a few drops of dye, making Tyrian purple extremely expensive. It was worth the cost, however; Tyrian purple was famous because over time its color would not fade but actually become brighter and more beautiful. As such, the citizens of Tyre were extremely wealthy.

[7] Genesis 37:6-7, "He said to them, 'Hear this dream that I have dreamed: [7] Behold, we were binding sheaves in the field, and behold, my sheaf arose and stood upright. And behold, your sheaves gathered around it and bowed down to my sheaf.'"

dream, the sun, moon, and eleven stars bowed down to him.[8] In this dream, the sun and moon represented their parents. Joseph's brothers were probably annoyed when their spoiled baby brother told them about a dream where they all worshiped him. But when his delusions of grandeur included their parents, and the actual sun, moon, and stars, they got *really* angry. Angry enough to kill.

In the ancient Near East, celestial bodies were powerful and mysterious entities, worshiped in their own right. It was as if Joseph was saying that the Palestinian gods bowed down to him. There is no wrath like an angry mob – unless it is an angry mob using religion to justify their actions. Like any mob, things got out of hand really fast, and soon Joseph was the one seeing stars.

The Conspiracy
It did not take long for the brothers' hatred of Joseph to escalate into a crime against him. While the brothers were out tending their flocks near Shechem, Jacob became concerned for their welfare and sent Joseph to check on them.

When Joseph's brothers saw him coming, they recognized him. While he approached, they made plans to kill him. A.W. Pink says, "The hatred of the brothers found opportunity in the love that sought them."[9] Verses 19-20[10] provide us with the brothers' plans as well as the motivation behind them.[11] Clearly, Joseph's brothers were upset about his dreams as they called him a "dreamer." Joseph's brothers may have been overreacting just a little bit. They were just dreams, after all. However, culturally, dreams were often considered to be prophecies. Indeed, Joseph

---

[8] Genesis 37:9, "Then he dreamed another dream and told it to his brothers and said, 'Behold, I have dreamed another dream. Behold, the sun, the moon, and eleven stars were bowing down to me.'"

[9] A.W. Pink, *Gleanings in Genesis* (Chicago: Moody, 1981), 357.

[10] Genesis 37:19-20, "Here comes the dreamer!" they said. 20 "Come on, let's kill him and throw him into one of these cisterns. We can tell our father, 'A wild animal has eaten him.' Then we'll see what becomes of his dreams!"

[11] John H. Sailhammer, *Genesis* TEBC (Grand Rapids, Zondervan, 2008), 274.

later showed his gift of translating dreams into reality. (I still cannot see dreaming as a way to justify murder.) Ironically, the evil they will bestow upon Joseph will lead to the fulfillment of the prophecy of his dreams.

The brothers' plan was a work in progress. According to verse 20, they intended to kill Joseph and throw him into a pit (a dry cistern) and tell their father that a wild animal had killed him. How badly would one have to hate his brother to actually murder him? John Calvin shows his contempt for Joseph's brothers' actions when he said, "But in profane history, no such thing is found, as that nine brothers should conspire together for the destruction of an innocent youth, and, like wild beasts, should pounce upon him with bloody hands."[12]

This is a great example of how a mob mentality can influence people to commit crimes out of their nature. Protected by the anonymity of a group, normal people will vandalize, loot, and burn buildings down. Or beat a stranger to death because of their clothing or race. Despicable acts they would normally *never even consider*. The brothers seemed to have a built-in mob mentality that, when combined with their apparent lack of conscience, frequently poured gasoline on a fire – like circumcising and murdering an entire town because someone slept with your sister.[13]

A Change of Heart
While the brothers all seemed to agree to kill Joseph, one did object to his murder. Reuben opposed the plot to kill Joseph and persuaded his brothers to throw him into a pit and leave him there. The pits were dry cisterns. Therefore, Joseph would not have drowned, but the cistern was deep enough to prevent escape. As the oldest brother, Reuben would have to answer to Jacob for Joseph's death.[14] So we don't know if Reuben's conscience was troubled or if he was just worried about the consequences.

---

[12] John. Calvin, *Calvin's Commentaries,* Volume I (Grand Rapids: Baker, 1993), 265.
[13] See Genesis 34 for the story of the "Shechem incident."
[14] Besides that, Reuben had to get back into Jacob's good graces after his little stunt in Genesis 35:22. (I won't print the verse here so you'll have to look this one up.)

Regardless, he secretly planned on returning to the scene of the crime and rescuing Joseph.

The brothers showed the callousness of their hearts when they sat down and ate a meal together while Joseph languished in the pit. Joseph had been left for dead. He would not have lasted long without food or water. While Joseph suffered, his brothers ate and drank, indifferent to their cruelty against him.

As the adrenaline of a mob fades, cooler heads prevail. This is where average people begin to experience shock and regret over their actions, or fear for the consequences. It is not merely Reuben who was having second thoughts about killing Joseph. Judah played a crucial role in saving Joseph's life. Upon seeing the Ishmaelite traders, Judah spoke up and talked the brothers into selling Joseph to slavers bound for Egypt.[15] Ultimately, the brothers reverted to the original plan and take Joseph's coat and cover it in blood to explain his absence.[16]

I cannot fathom what Jacob went through when his sons told him a wild animal had mauled Joseph, especially when there were no remains to bury. It is hard for a parent not to have their child's body for burial. Without a body, parents often experience a lack of closure following the murder of their child. Families of murder victims frequently remain vigilant for years or even decades in their efforts to recover their loved one for burial. Some cannot accept that the person is really dead. They express

---

[15] Critics of the Bible list the nationality of the traders as a contradiction of Scripture, which supports their claim that the Bible is untrue. The problem is that in various translations of Scripture, the traders are listed as three different groups of people:
- The Ishmaelites were descendants of Abraham and Hagar. (Genesis 37:28)
- The Midianites and Medanites were descendants of Abraham and Keturah. (Genesis 25:1-2)

So, which is it? Ishmaelites, Midianites, or Medanites? There are two explanations: The Ishmaelites, Midianites, and Medanites were all direct descendants of Abraham (within two generations). The three groups, because of the similarities in ancestry, traveled in the same caravan together. Another possibility is that the three groups were often confused because they resembled each other and had a common ancestor in Abraham.

[16] Here again we see how sin results in the shedding of blood.

recurrent thoughts about their final moments or obsess about finding their remains.

In the end, the bloodstained coat was all that remained of Joseph.[17] Jacob immediately recognized Joseph's coat, put on his mourning clothes, and grieved the death of his beloved son. Jacob had been wounded at the deepest level.[18] Genesis 37:35 says, "All his sons and all his daughters rose up to comfort him, but he refused to be comforted and said, 'No, I shall go down to Sheol to my son, mourning.' Thus, his father wept for him." Despite the depths of Jacob's grief, *the brothers remained silent on the matter for years.* That is the most egregious thing that they did. They never told Jacob what really happened or that Joseph might be alive in Egypt. While Jacob sat watching the horizon hoping against hope that Joseph would return, the brothers kept their evil secret and watched their father grieve for a child that was still alive.

Twenty Shekels of Silver
The Ishmaelites traded spices and slaves from the East with Egypt. Led by Judah, Joseph's brothers approached them and set up their transaction. They ended up selling Joseph for twenty pieces of silver. At the time, the price for a boy slave was between 5 and 20 shekels.[19] The price for an adult male slave was 30 shekels.[20] However, the Ishmaelites wanted to make a profit, so Joseph's brothers sold him for a reduced amount. It's despicable enough to sell your own flesh and blood into slavery, let alone to do so at a discount.

---

[17] Sailhammer, 275.
[18] Pink, 311.
[19] Leviticus 27:5, "If the person is from five years old up to twenty years old, the valuation shall be for a male twenty shekels, and for a female ten shekels."
[20] Exodus 21:32, "If the ox gores a slave, male or female, the owner shall give to their master thirty shekels of silver, and the ox shall be stoned."

God's Providence Revealed

After being sold into slavery, Joseph was placed in charge of running Potiphar's house. Potiphar was the captain of Pharaoh's guard. While serving in Potiphar's house, Joseph was falsely accused of sexually harassing and attempting to rape Potiphar's wife.[21] As a result, he was sent to prison. According to Genesis 39:22,[22] Joseph flourished in his role in prison where the prison warden put Joseph in charge of the prison and trusted him to take care of things. (We can see how events of Joseph's life were developing him as a leader.)

Genesis 40 tells us the story of Joseph interpreting the dreams of two of his fellow prisoners, the baker and the cup-bearer of Pharaoh. Sometime later, Pharaoh had a dream, and Joseph was brought from prison to interpret it. The dream predicted a devastating famine that would last seven years. Pharaoh was so impressed with Joseph that he awarded him with the number two position of authority in all of Egypt and tasked him with stockpiling food for the famine.

During the famine, his brothers came to buy food. Joseph was reunited with his brothers and had them bring their father and their families to Egypt to live in prosperity. God had used Joseph's suffering and trials to grow him into a leader and to place him in a position of authority to be able to rescue his brothers from death, even though they had wished him dead.

If you were wanting to see justice for Joseph in terms of his brothers' sins being revealed and their recompense received, you might be disappointed. Indeed, it seems that the brothers haven't suffered for their despicable crimes. But there is evidence that they haven't prospered in the interim. As shepherds, a famine means they have had to watch helplessly as their flocks, their livelihood, have suffered and died. They have worried that their wives and children would starve. Finally, they were humbled enough to have to go to a foreign country to beg for grain. Just as Joseph's

---

[21] Genesis 39:6-23.

[22] Genesis 39:22, "And the keeper of the prison put Joseph in charge of all the prisoners who were in the prison. Whatever was done there, he was the one who did it."

dream predicted, he had risen high while they have been brought low. Not to be missed is the divine irony that the brothers, portrayed as sheaves of grain in the dream, came to Joseph to beg for grain.

What about gaining their father's love? Remember that jealousy played a factor in the brothers' hatred of Joseph. Is there any evidence that Jacob's love was transferred to the erstwhile brothers? On the contrary, Genesis 42:36[23] shows us that Benjamin had become his daddy's favorite. So, their evil scheme failed entirely. Not only was Joseph not permanently harmed, but his elimination only transferred Jacob's love to Rachel's remaining son.

The Brothers' Response
In Genesis 50:20, Joseph explained God's providence in his life – how all the events of his life brought him to this point. "As for you, you meant evil against me, but God meant it for good, to bring it about that many people should be kept alive, as they are today." In looking back on the events of his life, Joseph saw God's providential hand moving to save the lives of countless people. Joseph could have chosen to hold on to his hurts with anger toward his brothers and God. But Joseph *chose* to see how his brothers' evil actions resulted in the saving of many lives. God, indeed, had taken these evils and used them for good.[24] This is a model for how we are to respond to the evil in the world around us. We can become bitter and angry, seek revenge, and commit murder in our hearts.[25] Or we can

---

[23] Genesis 42:36, "And Jacob their father said to them, 'You have bereaved me of my children: Joseph is no more, and Simeon is no more, and now you would take Benjamin. All this has come against me.'"
[24] Romans 8:28, "And we know that for those who love God all things work together for good, for those who are called according to His purpose."
[25] Some say that the brothers were not guilty of murder, but according to Jesus, they were guilty in their hearts. Matthew 5:21-22, "You have heard that it was said to those of old, 'You shall not murder; and whoever murders will be liable to judgment.' [22] But I say to you that everyone who is angry with his brother will be liable to judgment; whoever insults his brother will be liable to the council; and whoever says, 'You fool!' will be liable to the hell of fire."

submit our need to be in control to God and look with joy to see what good He will bring from evil.

We can see that Joseph's words and character run counter to his brothers and Joseph shows us how to respond to the world's hurts. But his brothers weren't through proving that even after being forgiven for their horrible crimes, even after being rescued from the agony of watching their children die from famine, even after being spared any more time of seeing their father grieve himself to the grave; their hearts remained unchanged. They were unrepentant.

After their father died, Joseph's brothers became worried that Joseph would seek revenge for selling him into slavery. Despite everything that Joseph had done for them - his words of love and forgiveness, using his position of influence to rescue their families, demanding no justice and exacting no punishment - they *still* didn't know who Joseph was. How could they even think that Joseph was plotting his revenge all along, until their father wasn't around to see his evil retribution? *Because it is what they would have done.*

Joseph's Christ-like love and forgiveness confused his brothers. They couldn't understand it. Joseph's brothers foreshadow the Jews in Jesus' time - the mob that screamed for His death on their holiest holiday. In the same way, the modern world does not understand us when we show Christ's love and forgiveness to them. Like Joseph's brothers, people will continue to treat us harshly, doubt us, and expect the worst from us. Are you surprised? You shouldn't be. Jesus told us it would be like this.[26] And just as Joseph's brothers never understood him and returned his loving-kindness with judgmental suspicion and cruel expectations, we should expect no less from the culture around us.

---

[26] John 15:18-20, "If the world hates you, know that it has hated me before it hated you. If you were of the world, the world would love you as its own; but because you are not of the world, but I chose you out of the world, therefore the world hates you. Remember the word that I said to you: 'A servant is not greater than his master.' If they persecuted me, they will also persecute you. If they kept my word, they will also keep yours."

REVIEW QUESTIONS

1. What, to you, was the brothers' most egregious sin? Why?

2. Define the mob mentality. What are some other examples of the mob mentality? Why is the mob mentality so dangerous?

3. Are there other Bible characters who are similar to Joseph's brothers? How so?

4. Consider Genesis 50:20. What other instances in Scripture did God work evil for good? Is our perception of bad and evil the same as God's perception?

5. "No good deed goes unpunished." Explain this common cynical expression. Have you ever felt punished for actions you intended for good? How did Joseph's brothers' thoughts and actions reflect this worldly mindset?

6. Consider the following verses and comment on how they reflect on how we are to live.

   Galatians 6:9

   Romans 8:18

   Hebrews 10:32-36

Moses and Aaron Before Pharaoh, Gustave Dore.
Engraving, 1866. Dore's English Bible.

3

Pharoah

EXODUS 1:8-22

Now there arose a new king over Egypt, who did not know Joseph. ⁹ And he said to his people, "Behold, the people of Israel are too many and too mighty for us. ¹⁰ Come, let us deal shrewdly with them, lest they multiply, and, if war breaks out, they join our enemies and fight against us and escape from the land." ¹¹ Therefore they set taskmasters over them to afflict them with heavy burdens. They built for Pharaoh store cities, Pithom and Rameses. ¹² But the more they were oppressed, the more they multiplied and the more they spread abroad. And the Egyptians were in dread of the people of Israel. ¹³ So they ruthlessly made the people of Israel work as slaves ¹⁴ and made their lives bitter with hard service, in mortar and brick, and in all kinds of work in the field. In all their work they ruthlessly made them work as slaves. Then the king of Egypt said to the Hebrew midwives, one of whom was named Shiphrah and the other Puah, [16] "When you serve as midwife to the Hebrew women and see them on the birthstool, if it is a son, you shall kill him, but if it is a daughter, she shall live." [17] But the midwives feared God and did not do as the king of Egypt commanded them, but let the male children live. [18] So the king of Egypt called the midwives and said to them, "Why have you done this, and let the male children live?" [19] The midwives said to Pharaoh, "Because the Hebrew women are not like the Egyptian women, for they are vigorous and give birth before the midwife comes to them." [20] So God dealt well with the midwives. And the people multiplied and grew very strong. [21] And because the midwives feared God, He gave them families. [22] Then Pharaoh commanded all his people, "Every son that is born to the Hebrews you shall cast into the Nile, but you shall let every daughter live."

GENESIS ENDS ON A HIGH point with the relocation of Israel to Egypt under Joseph's leadership. Four hundred years later, the book of Exodus begins, indicating that God has blessed the Israelites and they have multiplied greatly. However, following Joseph's time, the Israelites were no longer full members of Egyptian society and had been relegated to a lower class of slaves. They were not only seen as inferior to the Egyptians, but as Exodus 1:9 and 12 show, they were also greatly feared.

In Scripture, only two kings ever ordered infanticide: Pharaoh and King Herod the Great. Since these leaders commanded infanticide, they both are included in the Despicable Dozen. Pharaoh instructed the Hebrew midwives Shiphrah and Puah to do his dirty work.[1] In response to his "midwife crisis," Pharaoh commanded the Egyptian people to throw all Hebrew male infants into the Nile.[2] His lack of empathy toward the Hebrews was primarily motivated by his drive for power. The Hebrew people were becoming so numerous that they posed a threat to Pharaoh's throne.

The Office of Pharaoh

If you're like me, you've likely thought that the Pharaoh who ruled when Moses was born was the father of the Pharaoh who ruled during the ten plagues.[3] This was not the case. When Scripture speaks of Pharaoh, it is referring to the office, not the individual Pharaoh. It is similar to how we say "President of the United States" without referring to the president by name. The Pharaoh at the time of Moses' birth was Thutmose I. He was followed by Pharaohs Thutmose II, Thutmose III, Hatshepsut, Amenhotep II, Thutmose IV, and Amenhotep III. Many scholars agree that the Pharaoh during the ten plagues was Amenhotep III (1390-1352 B.C.). So, there were seven Pharaohs from the birth of Moses to the time of the Exodus. We will be looking at Thutmose I and his unjust order to slaughter all Hebrew newborn males. Ironically, Thutmose I became Moses' adoptive father when his daughter drew Moses out of the Nile River.

Pharaoh's Command

At the launch of Nelson Mandela Children's Fund, Mandela stated, "There can be no keener revelation of a society's soul than the way in which it treats its children."[4] As a general rule, Egyptian society valued children. Children held a position of importance in Egyptian society. This is in

---

[1] Their names are included in the text of this story because they are unsung heroes of the faith who, by their actions, merit being remembered for their daring efforts.

[2] By eliminating male progeny, Pharaoh was ensuring that the Hebrew women would marry Egyptians and eliminate the Hebrew lineage over time.

[3] This was one of the basic premises of Dreamworks' animated film *Prince of Egypt*.

[4] Nelson Mandela, Address at the launch of the Nelson Mandela Children's Fund, Pretoria, May 8, 1995.

contrast to other cultures at that time. For example, the Canaanite worship of Moloch, Baal, and Chemosh demanded child sacrifice. Exodus 1 paints a shocking depiction of Pharaoh's departure from Egyptian cultural values when he ordered the infanticide of newborn Hebrew boys. Therefore, Thutmose I's command would have been an embarrassment to the tradition of the Pharaohs and Egyptian history.

The primary motive behind Pharaoh's command was, like Herod the Great, maintaining his position of power. According to Exodus 1:7,[5] the Israelites were multiplying and becoming exceedingly strong. This should not have been an issue, since the Israelites were not enemies of Egypt. However, motivated by fear for his throne, Pharaoh told the Egyptian people, "Come, let us deal shrewdly with them, lest they multiply, and, if war breaks out, they join our enemies and fight against us and escape from the land."[6] Pharaoh claimed that the Israelite threat was an issue of national security.

Pharaoh was paranoid about the Israelites gaining power over Egypt. However, there was no indication that Israel would rebel or join together with Egypt's enemies. At this point, the Israelites had lived and prospered in Egypt for 400 years without showing any signs of insubordination to Egyptian authority. However, history is full of examples of leaders overreacting to a perceived threat where there is none. This is one such case. According to Exodus 1:9, Pharaoh said to his people, "Behold, the people of Israel are too many and too mighty for us."

There was a legitimate concern about the Hebrew people being able to overtake the Egyptians. In the Pixar movie, *Bug's Life*, the protagonist, Hopper, is discussing how the ants outnumber the grasshoppers, even though the grasshoppers dominated the ants. In a motivational speech to the grasshoppers, Hopper said, "You let one ant stand up to us, then they all might stand up! Those puny little ants outnumber us one hundred to

---

[5] Exodus 1:7, "But the people of Israel were fruitful and increased greatly; they multiplied and grew exceedingly strong, so that the land was filled with them."
[6] Exodus 1:10.

one, and if they ever figure that out, there goes our way of life!"[7] The same was true for Pharaoh. I can picture him saying, "You let one Israelite stand up to us, then they all might stand up! Those puny little Israelites outnumber us, and if they ever figure that out, there goes our way of life!" Pharaoh's paranoia, like Hopper's, seemed justified.

Pharaoh's initial plan was for the midwives to do his dirty work. In verse 16, he told the midwives, "When you serve as midwife to the Hebrew women and see them on the birthstool, if it is a son, you shall kill him, but if it is a daughter, she shall live." Pharaoh was not specific as to how the midwives were to kill the newborns; he just wanted it done. When the midwives disobeyed, the Israelites grew mightier and stronger.[8] Their disobedience became a matter of national security.

The Midwives' Disobedience
Verse 17 tells us that, "the midwives feared God and did not do as the king of Egypt commanded them, but let the male children live." Regardless, the fact is that the midwives feared the LORD more than they feared Pharaoh. The midwives distinguished right from wrong, and they refused to follow such a wicked command. The intentional civil disobedience of these two women changed the entire history of the Egyptian and Israelite people.

There are two possible reasons Pharaoh's evil scheme failed. Pharaoh, in verse 18 asked the midwives, "Why have you done this, and let the male children live?" Verse 19 provides their answer: "Because the Hebrew women are not like the Egyptian women, for they are vigorous and give birth before the midwife comes to them." According to the midwives, the Hebrew women were giving birth before the midwives arrived. This very well could have been because the midwives took their time in traveling to the home of a woman who was in labor. Additionally, the midwives' answer to Pharaoh could also imply that the Israelite women delivered

---

[7] John Lasseter, Andrew Stanton, Randy Newman, Ira Hearshen, and Don Davis, *A Bug's Life*, USA, 1998.
[8] Exodus 1:20, "So God dealt well with the midwives. And the people multiplied and grew very strong."

without the need for a midwife at all. Thereby, babies would have been born before the midwives arrived.

The midwives were not the only ones practicing civil disobedience. The Israelite women did as well, since it is highly likely that the Israelite women knew of Pharaoh's command for the midwives to kill all newborn baby boys. Many of them may have delayed calling the midwife, if they called at all. Once again, the Israelite women were giving birth before the midwife arrived. No matter how it happened, God dealt well with the midwives, and the Israelite women were fruitful and increased greatly.

Since the midwives practiced civil disobedience, Pharaoh took his infanticide a step further and ordered the Egyptians to drown all newborn male Hebrew babies. Verse 22 tells us that Pharaoh proclaimed to the Egyptian people, "Every son that is born to the Hebrews you shall cast into the Nile, but you shall let every daughter live." The Egyptian people would have unswervingly obeyed Pharaoh's nefarious command for two reasons: First, they believed that Pharaoh was a god in human form. Secondly, since Pharaoh was a god, absolute obedience was required. Pharaoh was determined to remain in power over the Israelites.[9]

Another instance of civil disobedience occurred when Pharaoh's daughter rescued baby Moses from the river despite knowing he was a Hebrew. Exodus 2:6 tells us that "When she opened it, she saw the child, and behold, the baby was crying. She took pity on him and said, 'This is one of the Hebrews' children.'"[10] Even within Pharaoh's household, his daughter believed his command to be wrong and was willing to stand up to him.

This shows us that both Egyptian and Hebrew people knew that Pharaoh's command was morally wrong. Historically, when leaders issue evil commands, people will follow the command despite moral objections that it is wrong. Fear can be a powerful motivator and most Egyptians

---

[9] It is ironic that an Egyptian god would have to resort to such unthinkable violence in order to remain in power. If he were truly a god, his power would have never been threatened.
[10] His circumcision would have confirmed his identity.

followed Thutmose I's edict. But some individuals stood up and proclaimed their conscience with their actions.

In the 1960's, Stanley Milgram, of Yale University, conducted a famous, but unethical, series of experiments exploring the lengths ordinary people would go to obey someone in authority. The subjects were asked to administer shocks of increasing voltage to a stranger, ultimately delivering what they believed to be a fatal shock.[11] If the test subject objected to giving the shocks, they were told that they must do it. There were no actual risks or consequences if they refused to administer a shock. The study showed that 65% of people were willing to kill a stranger when someone in perceived authority told them to.[12] Considering how difficult it would be to stand up to Pharaoh when the risks were tangible and considerable, the courage of these women is even more profound.

Civil Disobedience
The term civil disobedience, the non-violent and intentional refusal to comply with certain laws, is credited to Henry David Thoreau.[13] It is typically used when the law causes a moral crisis of conscience for an individual. The midwives, in disagreement with Pharaoh's evil edict, practiced civil disobedience by refusing to commit murder. Pharaoh's daughter practiced civil disobedience when she knowingly took Moses under her protection and made him her son. Moses' parents practiced civil

---

[11] The shocks were not real. The perceived recipient of the shocks was an actor, and though the subject could not see them, recordings were played of the victim screaming.

[12] Gina Perry, *Behind the Shock Machine* (New York: The New Press, 2012), 10.

[13] For years, Thoreau refused to pay his state taxes for three reasons: to protest the institution of slavery, the government's extermination of Native Americans, and the war against Mexico. In 1846, a Massachusetts constable named Sam Staples directed Thoreau to pay his back taxes. Thoreau refused and was taken to jail. In 1848, Thoreau gave two public lectures where he justified his refusal to pay taxes as a way to not cooperate with the government. In these lectures, he called on others to do the same.

disobedience in not killing Moses but did so by exploiting a technicality in the edict.[14]

History is full of examples of individuals standing up against their governments for laws they believe to be morally wrong. This begs the question "When is it appropriate to disobey one's leaders?" There are indeed certain times where civil disobedience is appropriate. For Christians, civil disobedience is acceptable when the governing authority mandates a practice contrary to Scripture. R.C. Sproul said, "If any ruler, whether it is a governing official or a governing body, a school teacher, a boss, a military authority, a parent, or anybody in authority, commands you to do something God forbids or forbids you from doing something God commands; not only may you disobey, but you *must* also disobey."[15] (Italics added.) A hypothetical example of this would be if an institution required physicians to perform abortions and Christian physicians refused to do so based on the sixth commandment.[16] Those physicians would have Scriptural grounds to disobey.[17]

According to the Westminster Confession of Faith 23:4, "It is the people's duty to pray for those in authority,[18] to honor them,[19] to pay them

---

[14] Technically, Moses' mother obeyed Pharaoh's edict. She did cast Moses into the Nile River. However, he was placed in a basket before being put in the river. Pharaoh's command said nothing about baskets or flotation devices.

[15] https://www.ligonier.org/learn/series/church-and-state/civil-disobedience# Accessed May 15, 2024.

[16] Exodus 20:13, "You shall not murder."

[17] Prior to the Dobbs ruling, there were plenty of medical schools and residency programs that allowed physicians to conscientiously object to performing abortions. By no means are doctors required to do them at these institutions. However, historically, there have been institutions that required obstetric physicians to perform abortions. When my wife was applying for her residency in OB/GYN, she was careful to select programs that either did not perform abortions or would allow her to not participate, and thus conscientiously object.

[18] 1 Timothy 2:1-3, "First of all, then, I urge that supplications, prayers, intercessions, and thanksgivings be made for all people, [2] for kings and all who are in high positions, that we may lead a peaceful and quiet life, godly and dignified in every way. [3] This is good, and it is pleasing in the sight of God our Savior."

[19] 1 Peter 2:17, "Honor everyone. Love the brotherhood. Fear God. Honor the emperor."

taxes and whatever is owed to them,[20] to obey their *lawful* commands, and to be subject to them for conscience's sake."[21] (Italics added.) The New Testament calls for civil *obedience* over and over. This means that even when we disagree with our leaders over certain issues, as a general rule, we are still to honor them.

Therefore, we must understand that if we intentionally violate a civil law, there will be consequences for our actions, and we must be prepared to accept those consequences. These may range from minor consequences such as fines, to arrest and jail time. A great modern example of appropriate civil disobedience is Rosa Parks' refusal to surrender her seat to a white passenger on a segregated city bus in Montgomery, Alabama, in 1955. She was arrested for disorderly conduct. Her civil disobedience led to the Montgomery Bus Boycott, which included over 17,000 people and started the civil rights' movement. Or they may face more serious consequences including death, as was the result with Dietrich Bonhoeffer, a pastor whose objections against the Nazi party's practices resulted in his execution. The Hebrew midwives are recognized by name in Exodus because their actions undoubtedly saved thousands of lives but also carried the real risk of death due to Pharaoh's displeasure.

Christians can refuse to comply with non-Scriptural laws. But what about those who don't follow Scripture? For all people, Christians and non-Christians alike, civil disobedience is appropriate when the civil authority enacts a law or policy that contradicts moral law. This is what occurred in Exodus 1. For centuries, Egyptian society held children in high regard. This all changed when Thutmose I enacted a policy of state mandated infanticide. Therefore, the refusal of the midwives to comply with Pharaoh's edict was moral and right.

---

[20] Matthew 22:21, "Then He said to them, 'Therefore render to Caesar the things that are Caesar's, and to God the things that are God's.'"

[21] Titus 3:1, "Remind them to be submissive to rulers and authorities, to be obedient, to be ready for every good work."

Civil Disobedience In Scripture

While there are many Biblical examples of civil disobedience, the apostles were frequently subject to the consequences of defending the gospel against the leaders of the day. In Acts 4:13-21,[22] Peter and John had been preaching the resurrection of Jesus and had healed a man. The Sadducees[23] arrested them and brought before the rulers of the Sanhedrin,[24] where they faced charges for their actions. Since the man that was healed was standing with Peter and John, the council could not discount his healing. Verse 18 tells us the council's response, "So they called them and charged them not to speak or teach at all in the name of Jesus."

Peter and John had a decision to make. They could obey the council and stop spreading the gospel, or they could continue to obey Jesus' command to "Go therefore and make disciples of all nations, baptizing them in the name of the Father and of the Son and of the Holy Spirit, teaching them to observe all that I have commanded you."[25] To Peter and John, this was a no-brainer. The command of Christ overrode the commands of man. They were willing to go to jail rather than obey a law which violated the higher law of God. In verses 19-20, Peter and John answered the Sanhedrin, saying, "Whether it is right in the sight of God to listen to you rather than to God, you must judge, for we cannot but speak

---

[22] Acts 4:13-21, "Now when they saw the boldness of Peter and John, and perceived that they were uneducated, common men, they were astonished. And they recognized that they had been with Jesus. [14] But seeing the man who was healed standing beside them, they had nothing to say in opposition. [15] But when they had commanded them to leave the council, they conferred with one another, [16] saying 'What shall we do with these men? For that a notable sign has been performed through them is evident to all the inhabitants of Jerusalem, and we cannot deny it. [17] But in order that it may spread no further among the people, let us warn them to speak no more to anyone in this name.'" [18] So they called them and charged them not to speak or teach at all in the name of Jesus. [19] But Peter and John answered them, 'Whether it is right in the sight of God to listen to you rather than to God, you must judge, [20] for we cannot but speak of what we have seen and heard.'" [21] And when they had further threatened them, they let them go, finding no way to punish them, because of the people, for all were praising God for what had happened."

[23] The Sadducees were Jewish religious leaders who did not believe in the resurrection of the dead.

[24] The Sanhedrin was the Jewish ruling council.

[25] Matthew 28:19-20.

of what we have seen and heard." Peter and John were clear – they were going to disobey the governing authorities by continuing to preach the resurrection of Christ.

In the very next chapter of Acts, the apostles were again arrested for disobeying the authorities because they continued to preach about Jesus. Verses 27-29 tell us "And when they had brought them, they set them before the council. And the high priest questioned them, saying, 'We strictly charged you not to teach in this name, yet here you have filled Jerusalem with your teaching, and you intend to bring this man's blood upon us.' But Peter and the apostles answered, 'We must obey God rather than men.'" Peter and John did not concede any ground. They were going to disobey the Sanhedrin because, as Peter said, they "must obey God rather than men." This is the litmus test of Christian civil disobedience. We must always obey God first.

Our Response

How are we to respond when we are faced with a decision similar to the midwives or Peter and John? Peter said it quite well, "We must obey God rather than men." Peter used the word "must." It is required that we obey God in such matters. When a ruler such as Thutmose I makes a law that forbids what Scripture commands or commands what Scripture forbids, we are to disobey that law. This is much easier said than done. It is easy to stand on our principles and God's Word when debating a friend or posting on Facebook. It is an altogether different thing to act on those convictions when real and potentially serious consequences are at stake.[26] That's what makes the midwives' actions so amazing. They knew that Thutmose's law contradicted the Egyptian tradition of valuing the lives of

---

[26] The previous example of a Christian physician refusing to perform an abortion downplays the stress my wife was placed under in refusing to participate in second trimester abortions during her training. She faced disapproval from her professors and peers, comments implying she was simply lazy and shirking. She was then assigned excessive and often unpleasant tasks as "alternative work." There will be consequences for civil disobedience, and we must be prepared to accept them.

children but, due to their fear of God, they chose to disobey this despicable command.

Thutmose I was not the first evil ruler and will not be the last. The inclusion of Pharaoh and his "midwife crisis" in Exodus is to help guide us and to encourage us if we face a situation that calls for civil disobedience. But the midwives' story does not end with their refusal to kill the baby boys. We are told that God blessed them and that the Israelites continued to multiply and grow strong in spite of Pharaoh's edicts.

Rosa Parks lived to see the fruits of her labors to eliminate segregation. Dietrich Bonhoeffer died without knowing how WWII would end or that the Nazis' crimes would come to face the condemnation of the world. We may not ever have such a serious issue to stand for or need to give our lives for our faith. But we can know that even when we are standing up for something small, God will honor us for our efforts and that our salvation will not be thwarted by the rulers of this world.

REVIEW QUESTIONS

1. What are the differences between civil disobedience and rebellion?

2. When is it permissible for modern Christians to practice civil disobedience?

3. What was Pharaoh's decision to murder the Hebrew boys based upon? What does this reveal about his heart? Which idols were prevalent in his life?

4. What are some minor examples of civil disobedience today? (For example, a supervisor at work tells you to report something falsely.)

5. What are some other Biblical examples of civil disobedience, and what laws did they violate? Did Jesus ever practice civil disobedience?

6. Consider the following verses and comment on how they reflect on how we are to live.

    Hebrews 11:35-40

    Romans 13:5-7

    Matthew 12:1-8

Joshua Punishes Achan, Artist unknown. Engraving, 1700. Bible of Royaumont.

4

Achan

2 Chronicles 2:7

The son of Carmi: Achan, the troubler of Israel, who broke faith in the matter of the devoted thing.

Joshua 7:10-26

[10] The LORD said to Joshua, "Get up! Why have you fallen on your face? [11] Israel has sinned; they have transgressed my covenant that I commanded them; they have taken some of the devoted things; they have stolen and lied and put them among their own belongings. [12] Therefore the people of Israel cannot stand before their enemies. They turn their backs

before their enemies, because they have become devoted for destruction. I will be with you no more, unless you destroy the devoted things from among you. ¹³ *Get up! Consecrate the people and say, 'Consecrate yourselves for tomorrow; for thus says the LORD, God of Israel, "There are devoted things in your midst, O Israel. You cannot stand before your enemies until you take away the devoted things from among you."* ¹⁴ *In the morning therefore you shall be brought nearby your tribes. And the tribe that the LORD takes by lot shall come nearby clans. And the clan that the LORD takes shall come nearby households. And the household that the LORD takes shall come near man by man.* ¹⁵ *And he who is taken with the devoted things shall be burned with fire, he and all that he has, because he has transgressed the covenant of the LORD, and because he has done an outrageous thing in Israel.'"*

¹⁶ *So Joshua rose early in the morning and brought Israel near tribe by tribe, and the tribe of Judah was taken.* ¹⁷ *And he brought near the clans of Judah, and the clan of the Zerahites was taken. And he brought near the clan of the Zerahites man by man, and Zabdi was taken.* ¹⁸ *And he brought near his household man by man, and Achan the son of Carmi, son of Zabdi, son of Zerah, of the tribe of Judah, was taken.* ¹⁹ *Then Joshua said to Achan, "My son, give glory to the LORD God of Israel and give praise to Him. And tell me now what you have done; do not hide it from me."* ²⁰ *And Achan answered Joshua, "Truly I have sinned against the LORD God of Israel, and this is what I did:* ²¹ *when I saw among the spoil a beautiful cloak from Shinar, and 200 shekels of silver, and a bar of gold weighing 50 shekels, then I coveted them and took them. And see, they are hidden in the earth inside my tent, with the silver underneath."*

²² *So Joshua sent messengers, and they ran to the tent; and behold, it was hidden in his tent with the silver underneath.* ²³ *And they took them out of the tent and brought them to Joshua and to all the people of Israel. And they laid them down before the LORD.* ²⁴ *And Joshua and all Israel with him took Achan the son of Zerah, and the silver and the cloak and the bar of gold, and his sons and daughters and his oxen and donkeys and sheep*

and his tent and all that he had. And they brought them up to the Valley of Achor. ²⁵ And Joshua said, "Why did you bring trouble on us? The LORD brings trouble on you today." And all Israel stoned him with stones. They burned them with fire and stoned them with stones. ²⁶ And they raised over him a great heap of stones that remains to this day. Then the LORD turned from His burning anger. Therefore, to this day the name of that place is called the Valley of Achor.

ACHAN'S[1] SHORT AND TROUBLING TALE begins with Israel fresh from its victory over Jericho, where not a single Israelite soldier died in battle. God had commanded Israel that "the city and all that is within it shall be devoted to the LORD for destruction." (Joshua 6:17) The Israelites obeyed God by destroying the city and killing every living thing inside the city (except for Rahab and her family) and destroying all their belongings. Well, almost...

It's important to note that this was contrary to practices of the time, when armies routinely took slaves and plundered loot as their "wages" in battle. Indeed, destroying Jericho must have shocked the Israelites – it was rare for someone to destroy well-established cities. Standard practice was to occupy the city and assume all of the goods, including food, flocks, and herds. Jericho must have looked pretty good to a nation of people who had lived their entire lives wandering in the Sinai wilderness, living in tents.

After the battle of Jericho, Israel attacked the small Canaanite town of Ai. Ai was so small that Israel only used 3,000 soldiers to attack it. This should have been an easy win for the Hebrew army. However, when the

---

[1] Achan is a descendant of Judah through his incestuous encounter with Tamar, which produced twins Perez and Zerah.

dust settled, Israel was defeated and 36 Hebrew soldiers were dead. Joshua 7:5 describes the reaction of the Hebrew people, "Their hearts melted, and they became like water."

After Israel lost such an easy battle, Joshua was understandably distressed. He was concerned that other nations would hear of the defeat and surround Israel and wipe them out. He also knew the inhabitants of Canaan had heard about the crossing of the Red Sea and the victories against Sihon, Og, and Jericho.[2] The Canaanites feared God, and Joshua did not want God's reputation tarnished. But Joshua's concerns included an understanding that God allowing the battle to be lost signified that something was deeply wrong. And he wanted to know why.

Joshua had missed a significant requirement of God's command to the Israelites. The issue was that God demanded complete holiness from Israel.[3] If God was to dwell in the Israelite camp, the camp must be pure.

Devoted to the LORD for Destruction

One way that God accomplished the purity of Israel was by purifying the land of Canaan. The concept of being devoted to the LORD for destruction or "devoted to the ban" is found in Joshua 6:17, which tells us, "And the city and all that is within it shall be devoted to the LORD for destruction. Only Rahab the prostitute and all who are with her in her house shall live, because she hid the messengers whom we sent." The Hebrew word for "devoted to the ban" is *haram. Haram* is holy-war terminology in which unholy things are destroyed as a sacrifice to the LORD. Every living thing would be killed when a city was devoted to the ban. The only things that could be taken from cities devoted to the ban were gold, silver, and precious jewels. These things were off-limits as they were dedicated to God to be used in His temple. God had instructed Israel to devote four

---

[2] The story of the defeat of Sihon and Og can be found in Numbers 21:21-35.
[3] Leviticus 11:45, "For I am the LORD who brought you up out of the land of Egypt to be your God. You shall therefore be holy, for I am holy."

Canaanite cities to the ban: Jericho (Joshua 6:1-27), Ai (Joshua 8:26),[4] Makkedh (Joshua 10:28),[5] and Hazor (Joshua 11:11.)[6]

How could a just God order the destruction of entire cities? Was this genocide? These questions must be answered in light of Scripture, not by our modern presuppositions of justice and ethics. What might seem like a random act of violence was, in fact, a long-awaited divine punishment.[7] This was not indiscriminate killing. When we look at historical examples of genocide, they are typically an unjustified complete destruction of a people. In this case, the people that were going to be destroyed were not innocent. The Amorites and Canaanites that God commanded Israel to destroy were genuinely evil. They practiced idolatry, sexual sin, and child sacrifice. This cleansing of the land was important because it showed that God will not allow injustice to continue forever. God will punish every sin. In destroying Jericho, God displayed the overflowing cup of His wrath.

Despite doing God's work, Israel was no more righteous than those devoted to destruction. Deuteronomy 9:4-7[8] tells us Israel would possess the land but not because of their righteousness. Instead, God would allow

---

[4] Joshua 8:26, "But Joshua did not draw back his hand with which he stretched out the javelin until he had devoted all the inhabitants of Ai to destruction."

[5] Joshua 10:28, "As for Makkedah, Joshua captured it on that day and struck it, and its king, with the edge of the sword. He devoted to destruction every person in it; he left none remaining. And he did to the king of Makkedah just as he had done to the king of Jericho."

[6] Joshua 11:11, "And they struck with the sword all who were in it, devoting them to destruction; there was none left that breathed. And he burned Hazor with fire."

[7] For example, Genesis 15:16 discusses the iniquity of the Amorites when God says to Moses, "the iniquity of the Amorites is not yet complete."

[8] Deuteronomy 9:4-7, "Do not say in your heart, after the LORD your God has thrust them out before you, 'It is because of my righteousness that the LORD has brought me in to possess this land,' whereas it is because of the wickedness of these nations that the LORD is driving them out before you. [5] Not because of your righteousness or the uprightness of your heart are you going in to possess their land, but because of the wickedness of these nations the LORD your God is driving them out from before you, and that He may confirm the word that the LORD swore to your fathers, to Abraham, to Isaac, and to Jacob. [6] 'Know, therefore, that the LORD your God is not giving you this good land to possess because of your righteousness, for you are a stubborn people. [7] Remember and do not forget how you provoked the LORD your God to wrath in the wilderness. From the day you came out of the land of Egypt until you came to this place, you have been rebellious against the LORD.'"

them to possess the land as divine judgment on His enemies. God's command also shows us that the land belonged to Him.[9] It is His prerogative to give the land to whomever He wants.

Israel's conquest of the Promised Land was not genocide because God showed mercy to some. God always makes provision for the sojourner in His laws.[10] One such example of this occurred in Jericho with Rahab and her family. God was perfectly justified in His command to devote certain cities to destruction. But in His mercy, an exception was made for Rahab. Additionally, the entire Promised Land was not devoted to the ban.[11]

Achan's disobedience betrayed the fact that he did not understand Israel's role in exacting justice to God's enemies who occupied the Promised Land. Achan did not understand the need to cleanse Canaan from these ungodly influences before Israel occupied the land. This would be like children wanting to swim in a pool that has not been chlorinated. The water may look great to them, but swimming in it could make them ill.[12] As parents, we know that the pool must be cleaned before they get to swim.

In this, Achan represents the "every man" soldier of Israel's army. They saw destruction of valuable property and didn't understand. They saw all the inhabitants of one of the most beautiful cities of the ancient world killed, and yet God did not intend the houses, markets, and wells for them. They must have been confused.

A scorched-earth policy is a common practice of retreating armies. Burning everything to the ground is a strategy of leaving nothing useful for the enemy as well as making a victory hollow. Who wants to occupy a wasteland? In this, the soldiers' confusion was understandable in that victorious armies never destroyed the land they intended to occupy.

---

[9] This idea is alluded to more than fifty times in Joshua.

[10] Abraham's nephew Lot and his family were an exception to God's destruction of Sodom and Gomorrah. (See Genesis 19.)

[11] The Book of Joshua lists 31 cities that were captured. Of those 31, four were devoted to the ban.

[12] Chlorine kills bacteria such as salmonella and e-coli.

Ultimately, Israel devoted around 10% of the Canaanite cities to the ban. Since Jericho was the first city Israel destroyed, did the soldiers worry God was going to do this in every city in the Promised Land? The soldiers may have doubted that God would provide for them, but Achan's doubt took that fear a step further. We know that Achan was covetous, and as such, he decided to take things into his own hands. He decided not to trust God to provide for his family. He found valuable items and stole his "wages" from battle.

Achan and His Sin

Achan's sin was keeping something that was devoted to destruction. Was what Achan had done so wrong? Did 36 innocent soldiers have to die as a result of his sin? Did his family and his animals deserve to be stoned to death and burned? This seems a bit extreme, but was it really? Was God overreacting to Achan keeping spoils of war for himself?

According to Joshua 7:21,[13] during the battle of Jericho, Achan "saw among the spoil a beautiful cloak from Shinar, and 200 shekels of silver, and a bar of gold weighing 50 shekels, coveted them and took them." He then buried the loot beneath his tent. Achan knew God had commanded all of Jericho be devoted to the ban. He knew it was wrong and he didn't want anyone to see what he had done.

This is a human process we are all familiar with. We are all enticed by our sinful natures and led into sin.[14] But immediately, our hearts convict us of our sin. We have two choices at that point: confess our sins to God and receive His forgiveness… or harden our hearts and cover it up. Just like Achan, the spoils of our sins often end up like worthless garbage,

---

[13] Joshua 7:21, "Achan said, 'When I saw among the spoil a beautiful cloak from Shinar, and 200 shekels of silver, and a bar of gold weighing 50 shekels, then I coveted them and took them. And see, they are hidden in the earth inside my tent, with the silver underneath.'"

[14] James 1:13-15, "When tempted, no one should say, 'God is tempting me.' For God cannot be tempted by evil, nor does he tempt anyone; [14] but each person is tempted when they are dragged away by their own evil desire and enticed. [15] Then, after desire has conceived, it gives birth to sin; and sin, when it is full-grown, gives birth to death."

shamefully buried and hidden. Achan's despicable actions proved his guilty conscience and how he wanted to hide his shame from God and others.

Did Achan really hide his sin? Surely others knew what he did. If nobody noticed him carrying the spoils of war back to his tent, surely his wife and children would have known. I can hear the conversation in my head, "Honey, why does the floor of our tent look like it's been recently dug up?" "I don't know. Weird, huh?"

What is the modern value of what Achan took? Scripture tells us that he took 200 shekels of silver, 50 shekels of gold, and a cloak. Today, the silver would be worth $1885 and the gold would be worth $42,636. What about the cloak from Shinar? Shinar was a city near Babylon - the cultural center of Mesopotamia. Anything from Babylon was fashionable and represented success and power. This mantle of Shinar was not an old shepherd's cloak, but likely, a costly garment of great quality. Just like modern fashion labels, a man wearing such a cloak would be noticed and considered important. The irony of Achan's theft was that he could never wear the beautiful cloak or spend his ill-gotten gains without everyone knowing where they came from. So, he buried them in the ground, hoarded away for a future that would never come.

But God did not allow the loot or the sin to remain hidden. Luke 8:17[15] tells us our sins will be revealed and all will be made known. We cannot hide our sins from God. And now the blood of 36 innocent men was crying out to Joshua to root out the corruption before the bad apple destroyed the entire lot.

Consequences

Did Achan's sin merit such a severe punishment? How did God respond to Achan's sin? Joshua 7:11-12 says,

---

[15] Luke 8:17, "For there is nothing hidden that will not be disclosed, and nothing concealed that will not be known or brought out into the open."

Israel has sinned; *they* have transgressed my covenant that I commanded them*; they* have taken some of the devoted things; *they* have stolen and lied and put them among their own belongings. Therefore, *the people of Israel* cannot stand before their enemies. *They* turn their backs before their enemies because *they* have become devoted for destruction. *I will be with you no more*, unless you destroy the devoted things from among you. (Italics added.)

There are two things to note about the above text. First, when God referred to the sin in verse 11, He did not refer to the sin as Achan's sin alone. He referred to it as "Israel's sin." Achan, in violating God's command, acted as a federal head for all of Israel, bringing the whole nation into the sin and resulting punishment with him. Joshua 7:11 explains that God allowed Israel to lose the battle to Ai as a direct consequence of Achan's theft.

Second, the sin was serious enough that Israel's relationship with God was in jeopardy. Again, the death of 36 innocent men is a horrific thing. However, nothing is more crucial than God's presence with His people. It was better for 36 soldiers to die than for God to "be with Israel no more."

Why didn't God just punish Achan? Did his family and animals have to be killed too? The issue was Achan's family knew about his sin, and they didn't confess it. This is evident by the repeated use of the pronoun "they" in verse 11. While "they" refers to all of Israel, it also refers to Achan's family. "They" were complicit and were as guilty as he was.

Verse 15 shows what God commanded: "And he who is taken with the devoted things shall be burned with fire, he and all that he has, because he has transgressed the covenant of the LORD, and because he has done an outrageous thing in Israel." God demanded all of Jericho be devoted to the ban. Everything was to be destroyed except precious metals and jewels. Since Achan took some of those things for himself, he and his family became like the people of Jericho. God demanded that they be devoted to the ban as well. This is why they were taken outside the camp and killed and burned in the fashion they were.

The lesson of Achan's punishment is that God's holiness does not allow for exceptions. For something to be holy, it must be fully set apart for God. Not some of it. Not most of it. All of it. Since God is holy, He demands holiness from his people. Leviticus 11:44-45 says,

> For I am the LORD your God. Consecrate yourselves therefore, and be holy, for I am holy. You shall not defile yourselves with any swarming thing that crawls on the ground. For I am the LORD who brought you up out of the land of Egypt to be your God. You shall therefore be holy, for I am holy.

God repeats the command to "be holy as He is holy" nine times in the Old Testament. The holiness of God must be maintained. How could the Israelites become holy again? God showed mercy to Israel in that He provided them a way. In verses 13-15, God told Joshua that someone had kept things devoted to the ban and that Joshua, as the spiritual head of Israel, needed to address the sin. God then told Joshua what needed to be done to reestablish holiness within the camp. As extra motivation, God said that they would continue losing battles until this situation had been rectified. God told Joshua that all the people needed to consecrate themselves then cast lots to determine who was responsible. Then that person and all their offspring and belongings needed to be destroyed, just as Jericho had been. Once Joshua and all of Israel had eliminated that which was devoted to the ban, according to verse 26, "the LORD turned from His burning anger."

Why did God have Israel go through the process of casting lots? The evening before, why did He have them consecrate themselves? The simplest answer is to allow Achan time to confess. But if we consider that Achan acted on a temptation they all faced, it suggests deep-seated sin in all their hearts. God wanted the Israelites to spend the night searching their own hearts and stand before Him as a people because they were all guilty. Secondly, it is part of God's nature to be gracious and merciful. Isaiah 30:18 tells us, "Therefore the LORD waits to be gracious to you, and therefore He exalts Himself to show mercy to you. For the LORD is a God of justice; blessed are all those who wait for Him."

If we know anything about the Israelites, it's that they liked to complain. The only thing as predictable as their turning from God to sin was their grumbling. I surmise that Achan's sinful actions reflected a pervasive doubt of God's love and provision. Before they continued in their conquest of the Promised Land, they needed to be wholly committed to God's will. Achan and his spoils of war reflected the sin that needed to be eradicated from all of their hearts.

Achan's story shows us the lengths that God will go to keep his people from sin. *God demands holiness because He is holy.* God cannot be present where sin is. In his sin, Achan put his selfish desires before his loyalty to his country, his commander, and his God. He committed idolatry by placing his wants and desires ahead of the commands of God. Not only did his actions affect his family, but they also affected the lives and families of 36 Hebrew soldiers. When we sin, our sin has consequences on those around us. The lesson for Israel was that God demands holiness. It appears that the Israelites learned this lesson, at least for a while. (King Saul committed the same sin in the battle with the Amorites.)[16]

Rooting Out Corruption

The real problem with Achan, and likely all the soldiers, is that their hearts were not right with God. However, Achan followed his sinful heart and took his doubt of God's provision a step further. His greed reflected a sinful heart that was not committed to following God. His sin led others away from God into destruction.

Achan's story is not an antiquated cautionary tale. We face the same fears and temptations ourselves. Do you lie to cover up the shame for your

---

[16] 1 Samuel 15. Also, see chapter 6.

sins or inadequacies? Are you tempted to withhold your tithe when money is tight? Do you vent your frustrations with a brother or do you follow Christ's command in Matthew 18 to meet with them personally? When we allow fear to rule our hearts, sin can take hold and corrupt us. A heart full of sin and fear cannot be full of God.

God did not allow Israel to defeat Ai because their hearts were not right. Achan's sin was the outward expression of the sin in their hearts. God would not allow things to go well for them while their hearts were full of sin. Have you ever felt that God wasn't letting things go well with you? Things were not going right in an area of your life and you felt a sense of disquiet because the cause was something more than random events? It is a feeling almost like walking against the wind. It can be hard to hear the Holy Spirit whispering to you amidst the cacophony of noise of family, home, work, or school, much less the sin that threatens to ensnare and devour. When facing frustration or setbacks, we need to cease our striving and seek God's face in prayer and His Word. Is there sin holding you back? Are you holding on to false idols that you need to let go of? Are there fears controlling you that you need to surrender to God? Sometimes we need to dig up the floors of our tents and expose our sinful hearts.

We are all guilty of sin and deserve eternal separation from God. On this side of heaven, we never become completely holy. The stoning of Achan's family was the blood price that had to be paid to restore Israel to God's holy presence. Like Achan, restoring our holiness also requires a blood sacrifice. Executing God's punishment on women, children, and animals got Israel's attention. But that sacrifice pales in comparison to our sinless Savior's death on the cross. We can only become holy through the blood of Jesus Christ, who lived a perfect life in our place. When God judges us, He looks at His sinless, spotless, and holy Son and treats us as holy. We should respond in gratitude that because of Christ's sacrifice, God no longer needs to punish us the way He punished Achan.

REVIEW QUESTIONS

1. Do you agree with Achan's inclusion in *The Despicable Dozen*? Why or why not?

2. What did it mean for cities or people to be "devoted to the ban?"

3. God obviously knew who was guilty. Why did God make Israel go through the process of casting lots and sorting through a million people to identify the guilty party?

4. We are taught from a young age not to tattle on others. Is this always the right thing to do? How does the sin of others affect us? Are we as guilty as the sinner if we cover up their sin?

5. Genesis 3 describes how Adam and Eve sinned and, like Achan, tried to hide from God. Compare and contrast their actions with Achan's. How did God punish their sins? In your opinion, in these accounts was God consistent in punishing sin?

6. What is the immediate consequence of sin on our relationship with God? What does the Bible show is consistently required to restore His people to relationship with Him?

7. God's instructions to Joshua for identifying the sin and eliminating it from the camp are a road map for how to deal with sin in our own lives. What three steps did Israel take to prepare, identify and eliminate the sin from the camp? (See verses 13-15) How could you use this as a guide to identifying and eliminating sin in your life?

8. What does it mean that Achan functioned as a "federal head" for all of Israel when he stole the spoils from Jericho? Read Romans 5 and compare how Adam is described as the federal head for sin entering all mankind.

9. Consider the following verses and comment on how they reflect on how we are to live.

   2 Timothy 2:21-22

   2 Timothy 3:16-17

   Hebrews 4:1-13

Samson and Delilah, Anton Van Dyck. Painting: oil on canvas, 1629.
Venice: Kunsthistorisches Museum.

5

Delilah

JUDGES 16:4-22

After this he loved a woman in the Valley of Sorek, whose name was Delilah. ⁵ And the lords of the Philistines came up to her and said to her, "Seduce him, and see where his great strength lies, and by what means we may overpower him, that we may bind him to humble him. And we will each give you 1,100 pieces of silver." ⁶ So Delilah said to Samson, "Please tell me where your great strength lies, and how you might be bound, that one could subdue you."

⁷ Samson said to her, "If they bind me with seven fresh bowstrings that have not been dried, then I shall become weak and be like any other man." ⁸ Then the lords of the Philistines brought up to her seven fresh bowstrings that had not been dried, and she bound him with them. ⁹ Now she had men lying in ambush in an inner chamber. And she said to him, "The Philistines are upon you, Samson!" But he snapped the bowstrings, as a thread of flax snaps when it touches the fire. So, the secret of his strength was not known.

¹⁰ Then Delilah said to Samson, "Behold, you have mocked me and told me lies. Please tell me how you might be bound." ¹¹ And he said to her, "If they bind me with new ropes that have not been used, then I shall become weak and be like any other man." ¹² So Delilah took new ropes and bound him with them and said to him, "The Philistines are upon you, Samson!" And the men lying in ambush were in an inner chamber. But he snapped the ropes off his arms like a thread.

¹³ Then Delilah said to Samson, "Until now you have mocked me and told me lies. Tell me how you might be bound." And he said to her, "If you weave the seven locks of my head with the web and fasten it tight with the pin, then I shall become weak and be like any other man." ¹⁴ So while he slept, Delilah took the seven locks of his head and wove them into the web. And she made them tight with the pin and said to him, "The Philistines are upon you, Samson!" But he awoke from his sleep and pulled away the pin, the loom, and the web.

¹⁵ And she said to him, "How can you say, 'I love you,' when your heart is not with me? You have mocked me these three times, and you have not told me where your great strength lies." ¹⁶ And when she pressed him hard with her words day after day, and urged him, his soul was vexed to death. ¹⁷ And he told her all his heart, and said to her, "A razor has never come upon my head, for I have been a Nazirite to God from my mother's womb. If my head is shaved, then my strength will leave me, and I shall become weak and be like any other man."

¹⁸ When Delilah saw that he had told her all his heart, she sent and called the lords of the Philistines, saying, "Come up again, for he has told me all his heart." Then the lords of the Philistines came up to her and brought the money in their hands. ¹⁹ She made him sleep on her knees. And she called a man and had him shave off the seven locks of his head. Then she began to torment him, and his strength left him. ²⁰ And she said, "The Philistines are upon you, Samson!" And he awoke from his sleep and said, "I will go out as at other times and shake myself free." But he did not know that the LORD had left him. ²¹ And the Philistines seized him and gouged out his eyes and brought him down to Gaza and bound him with bronze shackles. And he ground at the mill in the prison. ²² But the hair of his head began to grow again after it had been shaved.

THE STORY OF SAMSON AND Delilah took place during the time of the Judges, which occurred between Israel's conquest of the Promised Land and the anointing of King Saul. This was the time, according to Judges 21:25[1] that, "everyone did what was right in their own eyes." Judges 14:4[2] and 15:11[3] tell us that the Philistines ruled over Israel, and that God was using Samson as a catalyst to start a war between the two nations. Philistia was different from Israel's other enemies in that they coexisted with Israel. Not only was Philistia ruling over them, but the Philistine occupation of

---

[1] Judges 21:25, "In those days there was no king in Israel. Everyone did what was right in his own eyes."

[2] Judges 14:4, "His father and mother did not know that it was from the LORD, for he was seeking an opportunity against the Philistines. At that time the Philistines ruled over Israel."

[3] Judges 15:11, "Then 3,000 men of Judah went down to the cleft of the rock of Etam, and said to Samson, 'Do you not know that the Philistines are rulers over us? What then is this that you have done to us?' And he said to them, 'As they did to me, so have I done to them.'"

Israel was amenable to the Israelites. Because of this religious tolerance, Israel was exposed to and began to worship Philistine gods.[4] When Israel entered the Promised Land, God commanded them to kill the land's inhabitants so that this problem wouldn't occur. Deuteronomy 7:2-5 provides God's instructions in this matter.

> And when the LORD your God gives them over to you, and you defeat them, then you must devote them to complete destruction. You shall make no covenant with them and show no mercy to them. You shall not intermarry with them, giving your daughters to their sons or taking their daughters for your sons, for they would turn away your sons from following me, to serve other gods. Then the anger of the LORD would be kindled against you, and He would destroy you quickly. But thus, shall you deal with them: you shall break down their altars and dash in pieces their pillars and chop down their Asherim and burn their carved images with fire.

Israel disobeyed God and failed to kill all the land's inhabitants. Scripture shows that even Samson intermarried with them.[5] And now they worshiped Philistine[6] gods. This is exactly what God said would happen. Scripture tells us that God is a jealous God, and He was angry at Israel's unfaithfulness. Exodus 20:5-6 tells us that "I the LORD your God am a jealous God, visiting the iniquity of the fathers on the children to the third

---

[4] The primary god of Philistia was Dagon. Dagon was the Philistine's god of crop fertility and the legendary inventor of the plow.

[5] Judges 14:1-3, "Samson went down to Timnah, and at Timnah he saw one of the daughters of the Philistines. [2] Then he came up and told his father and mother, 'I saw one of the daughters of the Philistines at Timnah. Now get her for me as my wife.' [3] But his father and mother said to him, 'Is there not a woman among the daughters of your relatives, or among all our people, that you must go to take a wife from the uncircumcised Philistines?' But Samson said to his father, 'Get her for me, for she is right in my eyes.'"

[6] The modern term Palestine is based on the word Philistine. Israel is still at war to this day because of their failure to obey God.

and the fourth generation of those who hate me, but showing steadfast love to thousands of those who love me and keep my commandments." J.I. Packer, in his book, *Knowing God*, sees God's jealousy as a "zeal to protect a love relationship or to avenge it when broken," thus making it "an aspect of His covenant love for His own people."[7] God would avenge this broken relationship and the interaction between Samson and Delilah provided the opportunity to do so.

Samson's Previous Interactions with the Philistines

If we look at Samson's life in view of Judges 14:4[8], we can see God's purpose in each of Samson's interactions with the Philistines. Interestingly, the pattern of violence and aggression grows more intense and reckless with each story. For example, Samson's marriage led to the deaths of 30 men from Ashkelon.[9] Samson's failed marriage led to him lighting the tails of 300 foxes on fire and running them through the grain fields and olive orchards that belonged to the Philistines.[10] This would have devastated the Philistine economy and further aggravated the relationship between Israel and Philistia. Additionally, the death of Samson's wife led to him killing a thousand men with the jawbone of a donkey.[11]

Another time, Samson was in Gaza, the Philistine capital, visiting a prostitute. Gaza had armed guards and a strong, fortified gate. The gate of the city was locked after dark for security, meaning those inside would

---

[7] J.I. Packer, *Knowing God* (Downers Grove: Intervarsity Press, 1993), 170.

[8] Judges 14:4, "His father and mother did not know that it was from the LORD, for he was seeking an opportunity against the Philistines. At that time the Philistines ruled over Israel."

[9] Judges 14:19, "And the Spirit of the LORD rushed upon him, and he went down to Ashkelon and struck down thirty men of the town and took their spoil and gave the garments to those who had told the riddle. In hot anger he went back to his father's house."

[10] Judges 15:4-5, "So Samson went and caught 300 foxes and took torches. And he turned them tail to tail and put a torch between each pair of tails. [5] And when he had set fire to the torches, he let the foxes go into the standing grain of the Philistines and set fire to the stacked grain and the standing grain, as well as the olive orchards."

[11] Judges 15:15, "And he found a fresh jawbone of a donkey, and put out his hand and took it, and with it he struck 1,000 men."

have to wait for first light before leaving town. The men of the city waited outside the gate to ambush Samson. Since he couldn't pass through the locked gates, Samson uprooted them and carried them 38 miles away to Hebron. The removal of the capital city's gates humiliated the Philistines.

Many of Samson's impulsive and violent actions were the result of his lack of self-control and his weakness for women. Why would God allow one of Israel's judges to commit such terrible sins? Judges 14:4 explains that God was using Samson (and his sins) to separate Israel from Philistia. Samson's weakness for women ultimately led to Israel's victory over the Philistines. The exposer of his weakness and the source of his downfall was a socialite named Delilah.

Who Were the Philistines?

The Philistines were a seafaring people who emigrated from Greece. In 1190 B.C., they invaded Egypt. However, when Egypt defeated them, the Philistines were allowed to settle up the coast in Canaan (the Promised Land.) This occurred during the Israelite conquest of Canaan. The Philistines established five cities: Gaza, Ashkelon, Ashdod, Gath, and Ekron. As the Philistine population grew, they overflowed into Israelite territory. Due to superior military technology, strength, and organization, the Philistines established dominance over Israel. They were finally defeated by King David around the tenth century B.C.

Delilah

Delilah's name in Hebrew means "delicate." According to Judges 16:4,[12] she was from the Valley of Sorek, which made up the Israelite/Philistine border. As such, Scripture does not state whether or not she was a

---

[12] Judges 16:4, "After this he loved a woman in the Valley of Sorek, whose name was Delilah."

Philistine or Israelite. In fact, Scripture doesn't tell us much about her at all. According to verse 5,[13] Delilah associated with the rulers of the Philistines. She was the original "femme fatale," a seductive woman who, through her charms, lured Samson into a deadly, dangerous, and compromising situation.

Delilah's behavior was driven by personal gain. She would be financially set for life if she turned Samson in to the Philistine authorities. Each of the five Philistine lords offered to pay her 1100 pieces of silver for betraying Samson. This was approximately 140 pounds of silver! According to Liz Curtis Higgs, that amounts to about $15,000,000 today.[14] (And to think, Judas sold Jesus Christ to the authorities for only 30 pieces of silver!) In addition to becoming wealthy beyond her wildest dreams, Delilah would also gain prestige. Not only would she become a "social influencer," but she would also become a national hero. The modern equivalent would be paparazzi following her around and her face gracing the covers of grocery store tabloids for years to come. This is what she had always wanted! It would be her dream life!

Samson and Delilah's Relationship
Samson and Delilah's interactions in Judges 16 are the textbook picture of a dysfunctional relationship. According to verses 4 and 15, Samson loved Delilah.[15] However, *nowhere does it say that Delilah loved him.* What Delilah loved was financial security and fame. She did not return Samson's love. Instead, she saw him only as a means to an end. Delilah's idols of fortune and fame destroyed her relationship with Samson. Yet, he

---

[13] Judges 16:5, "And the lords of the Philistines came up to her and said to her, 'Seduce him, and see where his great strength lies, and by what means we may overpower him, that we may bind him to humble him. And we will each give you 1,100 pieces of silver.'"
[14] Liz Curtis Higgs, *Bad Girls of the Bible* (Colorado Springs: Waterbrook, 2007), 117.
[15] Judges 16:4, "After this he loved a woman in the Valley of Sorek, whose name was Delilah." Judges 16:15, "And she said to him, 'How can you say, 'I love you,' when your heart is not with me? You have mocked me these three times, and you have not told me where your great strength lies.'"

was so smitten with Delilah that he ignored obvious signs of trouble in their relationship.

Four times in their relationship Delilah asked Samson the secret of his strength.[16] Did this not raise any red flags in Samson's mind? Did he not think that her line of questioning was peculiar and oddly specific? If you were dating someone who kept asking how they could best kill you, you would run from them. And yet, Samson seemed okay with her line of questioning. He didn't even flinch. [17]

Why then did Samson decide to play Delilah's game? He must have known what she was trying to do. Delilah was "delicate" as her name indicates. She was not a physical threat to him. Samson may have been motivated by his overconfident love of danger. Additionally, he may have been so addicted to Delilah's affections that he was in denial about her true motives.[18]

Another problem with their relationship was that Samson and Delilah were not honest with each other. Samson lied to her about the source of his strength. Delilah, while not lying, was keeping secrets. In verse 6,[19] Delilah was straightforward in her questioning. Each failed attempt to subdue Samson further embarrassed her. She was losing credibility with the Philistine rulers. After the third lie, Delilah had enough. She pouted like a child who didn't get what they wanted and manipulated Samson into revealing the real secret of his strength.[20]

---

[16] Judges 16:6, 10, 13, and 15-16.

[17] Did Samson's friends not warn him? "Dude, she's just not that into you."

[18] Was Samson and Delilah's relationship sexual? Judges 16:5 has the Philistine lords instructing her to "seduce him." The Talmud says that Delilah used sex to get Samson to reveal his secret, in spite of the fact that the biblical text only *implies* that the two had a sexual relationship.

[19] Judges 16:6, "So Delilah said to Samson, 'Please tell me where your great strength lies, and how you might be bound, that one could subdue you.'"

[20] Judges 16:15-16, "And she said to him, 'How can you say, 'I love you,' when your heart is not with me? You have mocked me these three times, and you have not told me where your great strength lies.' [16] And when she pressed him hard with her words day after day and urged him, his soul was vexed to death."

After days of Delilah's nagging, Samson came clean and revealed the true secret behind his strength. Delilah sprang into action, getting him to sleep on her knees.[21] Matthew Henry states, "When man sleeps, his greatest spiritual enemies do not."[22] Due to Samson's diminished spiritual state, he was vulnerable to losing his strength by having his hair cut. While asleep, she had his head shaved and God's strength left him. Matthew Henry continues, "Those who have left the Lord's protection make themselves easy targets."[23] Once the Philistines had him in their power, they gouged out his eyes and put him in shackles.[24]

The Final Chapter

At some point, the Philistines held a celebration for their god Dagon. This celebration occurred sometime after Samson's capture because his hair had time to grow back. Many bad decisions are made under the influence of alcohol. The Philistines were no different, for they were drinking and had the brilliant idea to bring Samson out of prison to the temple to entertain them. The crowd in the temple was well beyond capacity. There were over 3,000 Philistines on the roof watching Samson. There were even more people on the floor. Who knows, perhaps even Delilah was there, celebrating her ill-gotten wealth and fame?

There is great irony in verses 23-24[25] in that the Philistines claimed that Dagon had delivered Samson into their hands. In reality, the LORD used Samson's capture and imprisonment to bring about the Philistines'

---

[21] Jewish historian Josephus claims that Delilah plied him with wine to get him to sleep.

[22] Matthew Henry, *Matthew Henry's Commentary on the Whole Bible*, New Modern Edition. (Peabody, Hendrickson, 1991), 173.

[23] Henry, 173.

[24] Verse 22 is one of the greatest cliff-hanger verses in the history of cliff-hanger verses. Judges 16:22 says, "But the hair of his head *began to grow again* after it had been shaved." (Italics added.) Verse 22 is a poetic way of saying that God was not finished with Samson yet.

[25] Judges 16:23-24 tells us that "the lords of the Philistines gathered to offer a great sacrifice to Dagon, their god, and to rejoice, and they said, 'Our god has given Samson our enemy into our hand.' [24] And when the people saw him, they praised their god. For they said, 'Our god has given our enemy into our hand, the ravager of our country, who has killed many of us.'"

downfall. The entire drama of Samson and Delilah points to the climax in verses 28-30.

> Then Samson called to the LORD and said, "O LORD God, please remember me and please strengthen me only this once, O God, that I may be avenged on the Philistines for my two eyes." And Samson grasped the two middle pillars on which the house rested, and he leaned his weight against them, his right hand on the one and his left hand on the other. And Samson said, "Let me die with the Philistines." Then he bowed with all his strength, and the house fell upon the lords and upon all the people who were in it. So, the dead whom he killed at his death were more than those whom he had killed during his life.

The death of this many Philistines sparked war between Israel and Philistia, fought by King Saul and King David. King David conquered Philistia about 100 years later.

Delilah's Idols
Fame and fortune were Delilah's idols. Every aspect of her life revolved around them. They were the primary reason behind her relationship with Samson. She stood to gain considerably more money and higher social status by betraying Samson to the Philistine leaders. Delilah craved the limelight, and Samson was the one to help her get there. The promise of coming abundance caused Delilah to become indifferent to Samson and his fate.

One of Delilah's major flaws was that she focused on the stuff of fluff, that is, the inconsequential things in life – money and popularity. These idols seem valuable but are fleeting and have no substance to them. History has repeatedly shown us the hollowness of these false gods. For example, Martha Stewart was a prominent American businesswoman and television personality who faced legal consequences in her pursuit of wealth. In

2004, she committed insider trading. She was convicted of conspiracy, obstruction of justice, and making false statements to federal investigators. Stewart served a five-month prison sentence and faced financial penalties. While she was already famous, her indiscriminate striving after further financial gain led to her downfall.

There have been plenty of famous Hollywood stars who achieved fame and fortune, then found that it was not all it was cracked up to be. Jim Carrey once said, "I think everybody should get rich and famous and do everything they ever dreamed of so they can see that it's not the answer."[26] Statistics support Carrey's statement. Lottery winners frequently gain more money than they ever dreamed of. But nearly one third of them declare bankruptcy within five years of winning. They have so much money, and yet it is still not enough. It is never enough.

As we see in these examples, the gods Delilah so desperately sought after are still being served today. Our society, 4000 years later, is still obsessed with them. Look at reality television and supermarket tabloids – these false gods of fame and fortune are thrust in our faces all day, every day. The problem with these idols is that they don't deliver the satisfaction that they promise. According to Isaiah 44,[27] these false gods are profitable *for nothing*. Rudyard Kipling warned against them as well, "Beware of overconcern for money, or position, or glory. Someday you will meet a man who cares for none of those things. Then you will know how poor you are."[28]

---

[26]   https://www.goodreads.com/quotes/1151805-i-think-everybody-should-get-rich-and-famous-and-do Accessed October 1, 2024.

[27] Isaiah 44:9-11, "All who fashion idols are nothing, and the things they delight in do not profit. Their witnesses neither see nor know, that they may be put to shame. [10] Who fashions a god or casts an idol that is profitable for nothing? [11] Behold, all his companions shall be put to shame, and the craftsmen are only human. Let them all assemble, let them stand forth. They shall be terrified; they shall be put to shame together."

[28]   https://www.goodreads.com/quotes/6545539-many-years-ago-rudyard-kipling-gave-an-address-at-mcgill Accessed October 23, 2024.

A study by Rochester University[29] warns against the false gods that Delilah served.

> If you think having loads of money, fetching looks, or the admiration of many will improve your life — think again. A new study by University of Rochester researchers demonstrates that progress on these fronts can actually make a person less happy. "People understand that it's important to pursue goals in their lives and they believe that attaining these goals will have positive consequences. This study shows that this is not true for all goals," says author Edward Deci, professor of psychology and the Gowen Professor in the Social Sciences at the University. "Even though our culture puts a strong emphasis on attaining wealth and fame, pursuing these goals does not contribute to having a satisfying life. The things that make your life happy are growing as an individual, having loving relationships, and contributing to your community."

If we consider Delilah's actions in light of the University of Rochester study, the things she so dearly desired, money and fame, would not make her happy. In fact, striving after and attaining these goals actually made her less happy. The text details three specific arguments before describing her nagging Samson day after day until "his soul was vexed to death."[30] Proverbs 27:15[31] says a nagging wife is like dripping water, slowly driving you mad. Judges 16:6-17 certainly does not describe a peaceful relationship. Every minute of Delilah's time with Samson was consumed

---

[29] https://www.sciencedaily.com/releases/2009/05/090514111402.htm Accessed October 3, 2024.
[30] Judges 16:16, "And when she pressed him hard with her words day after day, and urged him, his soul was vexed to death."
[31] Proverbs 27:15, "A continual dripping on a rainy day and a quarrelsome wife are alike."

with her striving after her false gods. Fame and fortune make for dismal gods.

Is there anything that Delilah could have done to make herself happy? Yes, concludes the Rochester study: growing as an individual, having loving relationships, and contributing to her community could have made her happy. According to the study, she would have been happier having an honest, loving relationship with Samson rather than betraying him for $15 million.

If Delilah is not remembered for her wealth and prestige, what *is* she remembered for? Ironically, she is most frequently associated with betrayal and treachery. She is synonymous with being one of history's most infamous deceivers. It's about the despicable deed that she performed in order to garner fame and wealth. What a horrible thing to be remembered for!

Before we come down on Delilah too hard, how many of us, if placed in identical circumstances, would be tempted to make the same choice? 1 Timothy 6:10 says, "For the love of money is a root of all kinds of evils." This verse is often misquoted as "money is the root of all kinds of evils." However, money is not the root, *the love of money is*. And that was Delilah's problem. The context of 1 Timothy 6:9-10 provides a better analysis of Delilah's sin.

> But those who desire to be rich fall into temptation, into a snare, into many senseless and harmful desires that plunge people into ruin and destruction. For the love of money is a root of all kinds of evils. It is through this craving that some have wandered away from the faith and pierced themselves with many pangs.

Delilah's desire to be rich is what plunged her life into ruin and destruction. While there is no evidence in Judges 16 about her outcome, we have evidence of it today. She is known as a treacherous betrayer of the one who loved her. Her love of money took her from being the kind of woman she could have been to being complicit in the capture and death of one of the heroes of the faith.[32] This is what the love of money does to us if we let it. It takes us down roads we should not travel. Let us learn from Delilah and steer clear of the love of money, fame, and social climbing in our own lives. Grasping for this insubstantial fluff will leave us unhappy with empty hands and hearts.

---

[32] Samson is included in the Hebrews 11 "hall of faith." Hebrews 11:32-34, "And what more shall I say? For time would fail me to tell of Gideon Barak, *Samson,* Jephthah, of David and Samuel and the prophets— [33] who through faith conquered kingdoms, enforced justice, obtained promises, stopped the mouths of lions, [34] quenched the power of fire, escaped the edge of the sword, were made strong out of weakness, became mighty in war, put foreign armies to flight." (Italics added.)

REVIEW QUESTIONS

1. Why did God allow Samson to sin the way he did? How did God use Samson's sin to achieve His divine will?

2. What does Samson's prayer in Judges 16:28 tell us about how his experiences have changed him?

3. Why is money not the root of all kinds of evils while the *love of* money is? What is the difference?

4. Delilah's idols were fame and fortune. What impact do those idols continue to have on modern society? How are these idols more prevalent than before? Have things become increasingly difficult from the time of Samson and Delilah?

5. Samson and Delilah's relationship was riddled with dishonesty and secrets. How were they each guilty of dishonesty and secrets? What kinds of secrets are sinful between a husband and wife? How do you protect your relationships from these saboteurs?

6. Consider the following verses from the Sermon on the Mount and comment on how they reflect on how we are to live.

   Matthew 6:19-21

   Matthew 6:28-31

   Luke 12:15

Death of Agag, Gustave Dore. Engraving, 1866. La Sainte Bible.

6

King Saul

1 SAMUEL 15

And Samuel said to Saul, "The LORD sent me to anoint you king over His people Israel; now therefore listen to the words of the LORD. ² Thus says the LORD of hosts, 'I have noted what Amalek did to Israel in opposing them on the way when they came up out of Egypt. ³ Now go and strike Amalek and devote to destruction all that they have. Do not spare them, but kill both man and woman, child and infant, ox and sheep, camel and donkey.'"

⁴ So Saul summoned the people and numbered them in Telaim, two hundred thousand men on foot, and ten thousand men of Judah. ⁵ And Saul came to the city of Amalek and lay in wait in the valley. ⁶ Then Saul said to the Kenites, "Go, depart; go down from among the Amalekites, lest I destroy you with them. For you showed kindness to all the people of Israel when they came up out of Egypt." So, the Kenites departed from among the Amalekites. ⁷ And Saul defeated the Amalekites from Havilah as far as Shur, which is east of Egypt. ⁸ And he took Agag the king of the Amalekites alive and devoted to destruction all the people with the edge of the sword. ⁹ But Saul and the people spared Agag and the best of the sheep and of the oxen and of the fattened calves and the lambs, and all that was good, and would not utterly destroy them. All that was despised and worthless they devoted to destruction.

¹⁰ The word of the LORD came to Samuel: ¹¹ "I regret that I have made Saul king, for he has turned back from following me and has not performed my commandments." And Samuel was angry, and he cried to the LORD all night. ¹² And Samuel rose early to meet Saul in the morning. And it was told Samuel, "Saul came to Carmel, and behold, he set up a monument for himself and turned and passed on and went down to Gilgal." ¹³ And Samuel came to Saul, and Saul said to him, "Blessed be you to the LORD. I have performed the commandment of the LORD." ¹⁴ And Samuel said, "What then is this bleating of the sheep in my ears and the lowing of the oxen that I hear?" ¹⁵ Saul said, "They have brought them from the Amalekites, for the people spared the best of the sheep and of the oxen to sacrifice to the LORD your God, and the rest we have devoted to destruction." ¹⁶ Then Samuel said to Saul, "Stop! I will tell you what the LORD said to me this night." And he said to him, "Speak."

¹⁷ And Samuel said, "Though you are little in your own eyes, are you not the head of the tribes of Israel? The LORD anointed you king over Israel. ¹⁸ And the LORD sent you on a mission and said, 'Go, devote to destruction the sinners, the Amalekites, and fight against them until they are consumed.' ¹⁹ Why then did you not obey the voice of the LORD? Why did you pounce on the spoil and do what was evil in the sight of the

LORD?" *²⁰ And Saul said to Samuel, "I have obeyed the voice of the LORD. I have gone on the mission on which the LORD sent me. I have brought Agag the king of Amalek, and I have devoted the Amalekites to destruction. ²¹ But the people took of the spoil, sheep and oxen, the best of the things devoted to destruction, to sacrifice to the LORD your God in Gilgal." ²² And Samuel said,*

"Has the LORD as great delight in burnt offerings and sacrifices,
 as in obeying the voice of the LORD?
Behold, to obey is better than sacrifice,
 and to listen than the fat of rams.
²³ For rebellion is as the sin of divination,
 and presumption is as iniquity and idolatry.
Because you have rejected the word of the LORD,
 He has also rejected you from being king."

²⁴ Saul said to Samuel, "I have sinned, for I have transgressed the commandment of the LORD and your words, because I feared the people and obeyed their voice. ²⁵ Now therefore, please pardon my sin and return with me that I may bow before the LORD." ²⁶ And Samuel said to Saul, "I will not return with you. For you have rejected the word of the LORD, and the LORD has rejected you from being king over Israel." ²⁷ As Samuel turned to go away, Saul seized the skirt of his robe, and it tore. ²⁸ And Samuel said to him, "The LORD has torn the kingdom of Israel from you this day and has given it to a neighbor of yours, who is better than you. ²⁹ And also the Glory of Israel will not lie or have regret, for He is not a man, that He should have regret." ³⁰ Then he said, "I have sinned; yet honor me now before the elders of my people and before Israel, and return with me, that I may bow before the LORD your God." ³¹ So Samuel turned back after Saul, and Saul bowed before the LORD.

³² Then Samuel said, "Bring here to me Agag the king of the Amalekites." And Agag came to him cheerfully. Agag said, "Surely the bitterness of death is past." ³³ And Samuel said, "As your sword has made women childless, so shall your mother be childless among women." And Samuel hacked Agag to pieces before the LORD in Gilgal.

³⁴ Then Samuel went to Ramah, and Saul went up to his house in Gibeah of Saul. ³⁵ And Samuel did not see Saul again until the day of his death, but Samuel grieved over Saul. And the LORD regretted that He had made Saul king over Israel.

WE'VE ALL BEEN THERE. WHEN caught in a lie or an unfinished task, our sinful nature takes over, and we try to cover it up. We make excuses, deny, or blame shift. And if that doesn't work, we begin to apologize or attempt to avoid the consequences. We don't have to be taught how to do this. It just comes naturally. Some might be considered to be masters of dissimilation and plausible deniability. I am reminded of how my children used to perform their chores. One of the chores that we asked them to complete was to do the dishes. This is a very straightforward chore. (Much like verse 3[1] above.)

However, my children rarely completed the task. When the dishwasher was packed with dishes, they wouldn't run it, or even worse, they would leave a pan "soaking" in the sink. When confronted with the incompleteness of this chore, they often responded with, "I did what you wanted." After they were told that they had, indeed, not done all what was wanted, they shifted blame to another sibling. "Well, I loaded the

---

[1] 1 Samuel 15:3, "Go and strike Amalek and devote to destruction all that they have. Do not spare them, but kill both man and woman, child and infant, ox and sheep, camel and donkey."

dishwasher, but someone else was supposed to run it." Then comes their best excuse, "There is still room for another piece of silverware." They knew they had not fully completed the task, and yet they still tried to justify their actions. Even though we learn from an early age that making excuses when caught in sin doesn't work, in fact, it might worsen things, we still fight the desire to sweep our sins under the rug. King Saul was a master at this, enough so that he could be considered the "King of Excuses."

Saul was Israel's first king. He had been anointed by the prophet Samuel. Still his leadership style was impulsive and brash, and his lack of confidence and deep-seated need to please others made him susceptible to the influence of his people's opinions. He was further undermined by a lack of trust in God. When he was told to wait for Samuel to make a sacrifice, he got impatient and made the sacrifice himself.[2] He then made a rash vow in the middle of battle that no one would eat until Israel had destroyed its enemies.[3] This damaged his troops' morale and physical abilities and nearly resulted in the death of his son, Jonathan. But God gave Saul a second chance to prove himself. Samuel began by reminding Saul where his kingdom came from. He then commanded Saul to listen to God's words.

Amalek
The Amalekites were a nation descended from Esau, specifically his grandson Amalek. They were a nomadic people who occupied Southern

---

[2] 1 Samuel 13:8-12, "He waited seven days, the time appointed by Samuel. But Samuel did not come to Gilgal, and the people were scattering from him. 9 So Saul said, 'Bring the burnt offering here to me, and the peace offerings.' And he offered the burnt offering. 10 As soon as he had finished offering the burnt offering, behold, Samuel came. And Saul went out to meet him and greet him. 11 Samuel said, 'What have you done?' And Saul said, 'When I saw that the people were scattering from me, and that you did not come within the days appointed, and that the Philistines had mustered at Michmash, 12 I said, 'Now the Philistines will come down against me at Gilgal, and I have not sought the favor of the LORD.' So, I forced myself and offered the burnt offering.'"
[3] 1 Samuel 14:24, "And the men of Israel had been hard pressed that day, so Saul had laid an oath on the people, saying, 'Cursed be the man who eats food until it is evening and I am avenged on my enemies.' So, none of the people had tasted food."

Judah and Northern Arabia. When Israel left Egypt to come to the Promised Land, the Amalekites attacked them. When Israel was refused entry to the Promised Land and wandered in the desert, the Amalekites attacked them again. During the period of the judges, the Amalekites repeatedly attacked Israel. God decided it was time to punish the Amalekites for their repeated violence against His chosen people. He needed someone to do this bloody work, and the rough and tough King Saul was the man for the job.

God's command to Saul was specific: he was to kill *all* of the Amalekites.[4] This is the same concept expressed at Jericho - the very same command Achan violated. "Devoted to the ban" was not ambiguous or open to interpretation. Every living thing was to be destroyed. When Achan was discovered violating this command, he and his entire family were killed with stones and burned. Achan was punished for withholding a small amount of loot. Despite knowing this famous story and the severe consequences of violating this command, Saul brazenly spared King Agag and kept the best of the livestock alive.[5]

When confronted with breaking God's command, Saul made five excuses for his actions:

- Feign obedience - Saul claimed that he obeyed.
- Blame shift – Saul shifted the blame to others.
- Empty apology – Saul said he was sorry but continued to make excuses.
- Confess without facing the consequences – Saul admitted that he violated God's command, but didn't want to face the consequences for his actions.

---

[4] One issue that Saul faced was that the Kenites lived near the Amalekites. God did not command Saul to kill them. The Kenites were a clan that generally had a good relationship with Israel. They were related to Jethro, Moses' father-in-law. Jethro and his family had been kind to Israel during the exodus from Egypt. This is why Saul decided to spare them, and in doing so, Saul acknowledged the kindness that the Kenites had shown Israel. Since the Kenites were tent-dwellers, it was easy for them to move away from the Amalekites.

[5] If Achan is despicable for taking the little that he took, Saul is even more despicable.

- Refusal to change – Saul had made his choice to disobey, and he was unwilling to change.

While most of us have likely never faced such severe punishment for our sins, making excuses and attempting to avoid the consequences are as old as sin itself. In the garden, Adam blamed Eve (and God), while Eve blamed the serpent.[6] If we search our hearts, we will find that we offer the same excuses for our disobedience. Keep that in mind as we look at Saul's five excuses.

Excuse #1 – Feign Obedience

By worldly standards, Saul and his 210,000-member army had an overwhelming military victory. And Saul obeyed the LORD, *mostly*. After all, he and his army utterly destroyed all Amalekites, except King Agag. At the time, it was customary to spare the lives of enemy kings and demand a hefty ransom for their return. This protected a king in case they were ever captured themselves but was also part of the spoils of war. Sparing Agag in defiance of God's command, Saul could have been motivated by self-preservation, pride, and greed, as any ransom would have been paid directly to Saul. Saul's disobedience fell far shorter of God's command when it came to the livestock, with the text noting only the animals they despised or considered worthless, were destroyed.[7]

It appears that Saul was oblivious to his sin. Look at what he said to Samuel in verse 13: "Blessed be you to the LORD. I have performed the

---

[6] Genesis 3:11-13, "He said, 'Who told you that you were naked? Have you eaten of the tree of which I commanded you not to eat?' [12] The man said, 'The woman whom you gave to be with me, she gave me fruit of the tree, and I ate.' [13] Then the LORD God said to the woman, 'What is this that you have done?' The woman said, 'The serpent deceived me, and I ate.'"

[7] 1 Samuel 15:9, "But Saul and the people spared Agag and the best of the sheep and of the oxen and of the fattened calves and the lambs, and all that was good, and would not utterly destroy them. All that was *despised* and *worthless* they devoted to destruction." (Italics added.)

commandment of the LORD."[8] He was still riding on the emotional high of his victory. He had no idea that he'd done anything wrong, nor did he foresee Samuel was coming to chastise him for disobedience. He then detailed how he had obeyed the voice of the LORD. After all, he mostly did what God wanted.

God's command to destroy all the Amalekites, their possessions, and their animals had been specific and clear. Did Saul misunderstand what God instructed him to do? Sinclair Ferguson says, "Our problem in obeying God is not that we do not understand what He is saying, but that we do!"[9] Saul's explanation for sparing the livestock argues that deep down, he knew he had disobeyed. Regardless, his initial reaction to Samuel's accusation was to claim obedience.

Claiming obedience is denial in its worst form. Denial is a potent tool of the mind that protects us from truths we don't want to face. It can be so complete that we become convinced the lie is true. Saul, caught up in his delusions of grandeur, may have actually believed he had obeyed God.

In one of my favorite verses of Scripture, Samuel shuts down Saul's claim of obedience. 1 Samuel 15:14 tells us, "And Samuel said, 'What then is this bleating of the sheep in my ears and the lowing of the oxen that I hear?'" The proof of Saul's disobedience was all around them. He was to devote everything to destruction, including *all* the livestock. And what did Samuel hear? The bleating and lowing of animals was a cacophony in their ears, with each bray accusing Saul of disobedience.

When God commands us to do something as He did with Saul and the Amalekites, we must obey Him fully. God does not desire a halfway attempt at obedience. How do we respond when our teenager takes out the trash but fails to place a new bag in the can or folds the laundry but leaves all the socks unmated in the basket? We would immediately point out to

---

[8] It is interesting how Saul refers to God in verse 13, "Blessed be you to the LORD." He doesn't refer to the LORD as "my LORD" or "our LORD." He refers to him as "the LORD." This is indicative of his lack of a relationship with God.
[9] Sinclair Ferguson, *Man Overboard! The Story of Jonah* (Edinburgh: Banner of Truth, 2018), 12.

our children the unfinished tasks and ignore their claims of obedience that they did their chores. When God requires all, *most* is still disobedience. We are not to obey *most of* what God commands. We are to obey *all* of what God commands.

Aren't we all just like Saul? We claim that we obey God, but deep down, we don't. Do we claim to obey all of the Ten Commandments? Jesus addressed the importance of the condition of our hearts in the Sermon on the Mount. Many of us would never even consider murdering another person. But in Matthew 5:22,[10] Jesus challenged His listeners that if they had hated their brother, they were guilty of murder. In Matthew 5:27-28,[11] Jesus stated that anyone who lusts after another has already committed adultery in his heart. So, while we display outward obedience to God's law, inwardly, our hearts are far from Him. How many times each day do our hearts violate God's commands? Obedience is more than external. True obedience is obedience of the heart. Let us refrain from being like Saul and not claim obedience.

Excuse #2 – Blame Shifting

When Saul's claim of obedience failed, he switched to his second tactic: blame-shifting. Blame shifting is when you shift the blame for your sin to others,[12] the law, or the law-giver. Saul used all three forms of blame shifting: he blamed his army, directly and by peer pressure; he blamed the law that required the sacrifice, and he blamed God and His representative, Samuel.[13]

---

[10] Matthew 5:22a, "But I say to you that everyone who is angry with his brother will be liable to judgment."

[11] Matthew 5:27-28, "You have heard that it was said, 'You shall not commit adultery.' **28** But I say to you that everyone who looks at a woman with lustful intent has already committed adultery with her in his heart."

[12] Blaming peer pressure is another form of blame shifting.

[13] An additional form of blame shifting is very common in our culture: deflection. This is when you respond to being confronted with sin or mistakes by pointing out the other persons faults or bringing up their past sins, frequently when you felt wronged by them. This is very common in close relationships and is something we are advised to avoid in

Saul gave the impression that he was not responsible for his army's actions. However, nothing could be further from the truth. Historically, the Israelites were required to obey their leaders to the most minute detail. Since the LORD commanded Israel to devote Amalek to destruction, the Israelite army was obligated to do so. Israelite custom mandated that a leader was expressly prohibited from requiring obedience in violation of the law. The soldiers in Saul's army were required to kill all of the Amalekites and all of their livestock, even if Saul had objected. Furthermore, Saul did not redirect his army to devote every living thing to destruction when he saw them violating the LORD's command. Even though Saul was ultimately accountable for the Israelite army, he blamed his lack of obedience on them. If someone was in the wrong here, it was Saul. He did not stop the army's disobedience. In verse 24, Saul changed tactics by claiming peer pressure in that he was afraid of the people.

However, verse 21 tells us that Saul claimed the army "took of the spoil, sheep and oxen, the best of the things devoted to destruction to *sacrifice to the LORD.*" (Italics added.) By telling Samuel the animals were to be sacrificed to "the LORD your God," Saul attempted to shift the blame to the law requiring sacrifice, to Samuel, and to God.[14]

Saul is not alone in blame-shifting. We are all accustomed to blaming others for our own violations of God's law. How many times while driving have you disobeyed the speed limit because the other cars around you were speeding? We attempt to justify it by blaming the other drivers, "If I obey the speed limit, I will be a hazard." Or you might think the speed limit is too low for the road (blaming the law). Maybe you even think that the speed is that low only to allow the police to write tickets (blaming the law-giver). But, at the heart of it, you are still violating the law. Obedience to

---

marital counseling teaching the couple how to fight fair. While Saul did not use this tactic in this conversation, he did use it in the 1 Samuel 13:8-12 passage. See if you can spot him blaming Samuel for his sin by using deflection.

[14] As the king, Saul would have been expected to provide the animals for sacrifices of thanksgiving and praise. The more animals sacrificed, the better he would look to the people. But this is like seeking recognition for giving a huge church donation from stolen money.

the law is not subjective – it does not depend on whether or not others break the law. It only matters whether we follow the law or not. And if we violate the law, the responsibility is ours alone.

Saul failed to mention sparing King Agag, the responsibility of whose death fell completely upon Saul. Saul had no one to blame except himself for sparing the life of the Amalekite king. When Saul's attempt to shift the blame for his disobedience failed, he moved on to another tactic to wriggle out of his responsibility.

Excuse #3 –Empty Apology

In verses 22-23,[15] Samuel condemned Saul for his disobedience. Samuel explained to Saul that the LORD had rejected Saul from being king because of his disobedience. The verdict was in. God was finished with Saul.[16]

Saul's next tactic was to offer an empty apology, as found in verse 24, where he said, "I have sinned, for I have transgressed the commandment of the LORD and your words, because I feared the people and obeyed their voice." Note the continued justification and blame-shifting that follows the apology.

An empty apology is an apology in word only. It is an apology that is frequently followed by more blame shifting or justification of sin. Today, it is usually something like "I'm sorry, but…" As parents, we easily recognize empty apologies when our children offer a flippant "I'm sorry" when instructed to apologize. In management, we are taught to offer empty

---

[15] 1 Samuel 15:22-23, "And Samuel said, 'Has the LORD as great delight in burnt offerings and sacrifices, as in obeying the voice of the LORD? Behold, to obey is better than sacrifice, and to listen than the fat of rams.[23] For rebellion is as the sin of divination, and presumption is as iniquity and idolatry. Because you have rejected the word of the LORD, He has also rejected you from being king.'"

[16] God allowed Saul to remain king for a time but withdrew His favor from Saul for the remainder of his life.

apologies to de-escalate tense situations. A classic example is a manager telling someone "I'm sorry you feel that way." This statement is meant to acknowledge the other person's feelings but admits no guilt and offers no solution.

It was only after Samuel's condemnation that Saul confessed his sin. However, he still failed to repent. Saul displayed worldly sorrow instead of godly sorrow. As noted in our study of Cain, worldly sorrow says, "I'm sorry I got caught." Godly sorrow says, "I'm sorry I have sinned." Worldly sorrow involves the external appearance only. Godly sorrow involves the heart.[17] Saul's confession was due to sorrow over the consequences of his sin and did not reflect true repentance. He continued to make excuses to avoid those consequences, claiming he feared the people.[18] He confessed, but he still blamed the people.

Excuse #4 – Confessing without Consequences
After Saul's apologies, Samuel again informed Saul of God's judgment. In verse 28, Samuel told Saul, "The LORD has torn the kingdom of Israel from you this day and has given it to a neighbor of yours, who is better than you." Yet, even after this second rejection, Saul continued to attempt to avoid the consequences of his actions.

In verse 30, Saul confessed, "I have sinned." But this time, rather than blame others for his disobedience, he asked Samuel to honor him before the people. Saul must have been a pretty gutsy guy to ask the prophet of God to honor him immediately after being condemned for his sin. Saul was not concerned with the LORD or His justice, but only how he appeared before the people.

---

[17] An example of godly sorrow can be found in Psalm 51, which David wrote after he confessed his sin with Bathsheba.

[18] 1 Samuel 15:24, "Saul said to Samuel, 'I have sinned, for I have transgressed the commandment of the LORD and your words, because I feared the people and obeyed their voice.'"

Samuel had already explained the consequences of Saul's disobedience to him twice: "God has rejected you from being king."[19] These consequences would have been terribly humiliating. He didn't want anyone to know that God had rejected him. He preferred to carry on as if everything was the same. He wanted the people to remember that he was victorious in leading God's army in a rousing victory over the Amalekites. His worship at Gilgal would have been a public celebration with sacrifices to the LORD. Saul asked Samuel to go with him so that he might bow before the LORD, Samuel's God. It also shows us that Saul had rejected God as LORD. Saul was not concerned about losing a relationship with the God who made him king. Saul was only worried about saving face with the people of Israel.

Samuel likely understood Saul's true motivation to return to Gilgal, yet he acquiesced to Saul.[20] There are three reasons that Samuel returned to Gilgal with Saul and bowed with him before the LORD.

1. Saul was still God's anointed king. Even though God had rejected him from being king, his position demanded respect and obedience from his subjects.
2. Samuel's outward support of Saul was a means of God's protection of His people. Israel was God's chosen people, and the king was there to protect them. Saul was a proven warrior, and the people needed a king to lead and protect them from enemies. This shows us that God uses the unsaved to protect the His chosen. The same is true for us today. Our leaders may not follow God, but He still uses them for the good of those who love Him.[21] This is one

---

[19] 1 Samuel 15:23, "For rebellion is as the sin of divination, and presumption is as iniquity and idolatry. Because you have rejected the word of the LORD, He has also rejected you from being king." 1 Samuel 15:26, "And Samuel said to Saul, 'I will not return with you. For you have rejected the word of the LORD, and the LORD has rejected you from being king over Israel.'"
[20] 1 Samuel 15:31, "So Samuel turned back after Saul, and Saul bowed before the LORD."
[21] Romans 8:28, "And we know that for those who love God all things work together for good, for those who are called according to his purpose."

reason why the apostle Paul tells us to pray for those who lead us.[22]

3.   Samuel had to complete the task of devoting the Amalekites to destruction since Saul had failed to do so.

Again, aren't we all like Saul in that we often confess our sins to try to weasel out of the consequences? We want to get away with our sins without having to face the consequences of them, especially if those consequences are public. Saul begged Samuel to remove the consequences for his sin because he was worried about what his army would think of him. Oftentimes, the consequences of our sins are what God uses to bring us closer to Him. It is important to understand that even though we may have been forgiven, (in this case, Saul was not), there will still be consequences for our actions. We should accept those consequences as they are being used by God to work for our good.

Excuse #5 – Refusing to Change
Verses 32-35 provide the gruesome final details to the story. In verse 3, Samuel commanded Saul to devote the Amalekites to destruction. Saul had failed, and now it fell on Samuel to complete the task. He requested King Agag be brought to him. Agag came to Samuel in a confident, stately manner. Having escaped the sword of Saul, a man of violence, Agag thought he would be safe with this old prophet of the LORD, a man of peace.

Samuel declared God's justice in verse 33, "as your sword has made women childless, so shall your mother be childless among women." Sin demands justice. Samuel then proceeded to "hack Agag to pieces before

---

[22] 1 Timothy 2:1-2, "First of all, then, I urge that supplications, prayers, intercessions, and thanksgivings be made for all people, 2 for kings and all who are in high positions, that we may lead a peaceful and quiet life, godly and dignified in every way."

the LORD in Gilgal."[23] Samuel devoted Agag to destruction as the LORD had commanded Saul to do.

Saul's refusal to complete the execution himself is further evidence of his unrepentant heart. And this time, the consequences were very public. Murder crime scenes with evidence of overkill are telling to investigators, as they often reveal emotions and a personal relationship between the killer and the victim. However, Samuel's blatant overkill of King Agag was not due to anger or personal displeasure at having to finish Saul's work. Instead, the destruction of King Agag was making a point about how we are to obey God's commands completely and thoroughly. It was also a clear and shocking statement to the Israelites about Saul's disobedience and the removal of God's favor. Despite his rationalizing, blame-shifting, and attempts to save face, Saul, the "king of excuses," was humiliated in front of his people.

King Saul's inclusion in this book may seem questionable when compared to some of our other despicable villains. Compared to murderers and despots, his sin seems less egregious. But Saul's stubborn disobedience and blame-shifting didn't just cost him his throne, it cost him a permanent loss of God's favor. He remained unrepentant and more concerned with the opinion of men than with losing the blessing of God's favor. Like Saul, our efforts to cover up our sins and avoid public consequences will ultimately fail. We must confess our sins with repentant hearts and completely follow God. Anything less is just an excuse.

---

[23] There are a few words in Scripture that strike me as spectacularly vivid. For example, when the fish spits out Jonah onto dry land, the author uses the word "vomited," which connotes bile and other stomach contents covering Jonah as he exits the fish. The word "hack" has the same sort of color. Samuel did not neatly dispose of Agag; instead, he butchered him with his knife.

REVIEW QUESTIONS

1. Why was it so important to God that every living thing of the Amalekites be killed? Could this be considered genocide? Is Scripture justifying the destruction of Israel's enemies?

2. Look again at 1 Samuel 13:8-12 (the story of Saul making the sacrifice without Samuel.) What five forms of blame shifting does Saul use to justify his sin?

3. Do you feel that God overreacted by taking away Saul's kingdom for his sin? Why or why not?

4. Samuel executed King Agag in a very public and gruesome fashion. Why was this necessary?

5. Think of Saul's five different excuses. How do you respond when confronted with a sin or mistake? What type of excuse is your "go to" excuse? If this is difficult for you, consider asking a close friend or family member which one you use.

6. Consider the following verses and comment on how they reflect on how we are to live.

    1 John 5:3

    1 John 1:9

    Proverbs 12:22

The Death of Naboth, Caspar Luiken. Copper Engraving, 1712.

7

Ahab and Jezebel

———◦————◦———

1 KINGS 21:1-19

Now Naboth the Jezreelite had a vineyard in Jezreel, beside the palace of Ahab king of Samaria. ² And after this Ahab said to Naboth, "Give me your vineyard, that I may have it for a vegetable garden, because it is near my house, and I will give you a better vineyard for it; or, if it seems good to you, I will give you its value in money." ³ But Naboth said to Ahab, "The LORD forbid that I should give you the inheritance of my fathers." ⁴ And Ahab went into his house vexed and sullen because of what Naboth the Jezreelite had said to him, for he had said, "I will not give you the inheritance of my fathers." And he lay down on his bed and turned away his face and would eat no food.

⁵ But Jezebel his wife came to him and said to him, "Why is your spirit so vexed that you eat no food?" ⁶ And he said to her, "Because I spoke to Naboth the Jezreelite and said to him, 'Give me your vineyard for money, or else, if it please you, I will give you another vineyard for it.' And he answered, 'I will not give you my vineyard.'" [7] *And Jezebel his wife said to him, "Do you now govern Israel? Arise and eat bread and let your heart be cheerful; I will give you the vineyard of Naboth the Jezreelite."*

[8] *So she wrote letters in Ahab's name and sealed them with his seal, and she sent the letters to the elders and the leaders who lived with Naboth in his city.* [9] *And she wrote in the letters, "Proclaim a fast, and set Naboth at the head of the people.* [10] *And set two worthless men opposite him, and let them bring a charge against him, saying, 'You have cursed God and the king.' Then take him out and stone him to death."* [11] *And the men of his city, the elders and the leaders who lived in his city, did as Jezebel had sent word to them. As it was written in the letters that she had sent to them,* [12] *they proclaimed a fast and set Naboth at the head of the people.* [13] *And the two worthless men came in and sat opposite him. And the worthless men brought a charge against Naboth in the presence of the people, saying, "Naboth cursed God and the king." So, they took him outside the city and stoned him to death with stones.* [14] *Then they sent to Jezebel, saying, "Naboth has been stoned; he is dead."*

[15] *As soon as Jezebel heard that Naboth had been stoned and was dead, Jezebel said to Ahab, "Arise, take possession of the vineyard of Naboth the Jezreelite, which he refused to give you for money, for Naboth is not alive, but dead."* [16] *And as soon as Ahab heard that Naboth was dead, Ahab arose to go down to the vineyard of Naboth the Jezreelite, to take possession of it.*

[17] *Then the word of the LORD came to Elijah the Tishbite, saying,* [18] *"Arise, go down to meet Ahab king of Israel, who is in Samaria; behold, he is in the vineyard of Naboth, where he has gone to take possession.* [19] *And you shall say to him, 'Thus says the LORD, "Have you killed and also taken possession?" And you shall say to him, 'Thus says the LORD: "In the place*

where dogs licked up the blood of Naboth shall dogs lick your own blood.'"

THE STORY OF AHAB, JEZEBEL and Naboth is a classic tale of good versus evil. Naboth was a faithful Israelite vintner who had the misfortune of living next door to Ahab's summer palace. King Ahab, as Scripture tells us, was the most evil king Israel ever had.[1] His wife Jezebel was even worse, as she was a follower of Baal.[2] As a result, Jezebel led Ahab deeper into the pagan practices involved in Baal worship. 1 Kings 21:25 provides us with an accurate spiritual assessment of the king and queen, "There was none who sold himself to do what was evil in the sight of the LORD like Ahab, whom Jezebel his wife incited." In contrast, Naboth was a wholesome man of integrity who experienced horrible injustice at the hands of the evil royal couple.

The Vineyard
Our story begins with Ahab in Jezreel at his summer palace, when he noticed Naboth's vineyard next door. Ahab respectfully approached Naboth and offered to either trade or purchase Naboth's vineyard. What was Ahab going to do with Naboth's vineyard? Verse 2 tells us that he was going to use it as a vegetable garden.

In his defense, Ahab tried to do the honorable thing and buy the vineyard. Scripture doesn't say it was a bad deal. In fact, it may have been

---

[1] 1 Kings 20:29-33, "In the thirty-eighth year of Asa king of Judah, Ahab the son of Omri began to reign over Israel, and Ahab the son of Omri reigned over Israel in Samaria twenty-two years. And Ahab the son of Omri did evil in the sight of the LORD, *more than all who were before him.* And as if it had been a light thing for him to walk in the sins of Jeroboam the son of Nebat, he took for his wife Jezebel the daughter of Ethbaal king of the Sidonians and went and served Baal and worshiped him. He erected an altar for Baal in the house of Baal, which he built in Samaria. And Ahab made an Asherah. Ahab did more to provoke the LORD, the God of Israel, to anger than all the kings of Israel who were before him." (Italics added.)
[2] Baal was also known as Hadad, the Aramean, Phoenician, and Canaanite god of fertility. According to Jeremiah 19:5, Baal required child sacrifice.

quite lucrative for Naboth. However, Naboth refused Ahab's offer. Why? Naboth stood to gain quite a bit from this exchange. Ahab's proposal would have provided Naboth with financial security for the rest of his life. Naboth would also gain favor with the king. It sounds like a win-win. To Naboth and his descendants, though, the land was more than a vineyard, it was the family's inheritance. It had been in their family as long as Israel dwelled in the Promised Land. The issue was that God had specifically forbidden the Israelites from selling their land.[3] Land, to the Israelites, was physical evidence of the fulfillment of God's promises to Abraham. To sell the land would be to sell God's promises.

When Naboth refused Ahab's offer, Ahab behaved like a spoiled child. 1 Kings 21:4 reads, "And Ahab went into his house vexed and sullen because of what Naboth the Jezreelite had said to him, for he had said, "I will not give you the inheritance of my fathers." And he lay down on his bed and turned away his face and would eat no food." Vexed means annoyed, frustrated, or worried. Sullen implies depressed or gloomy. Ahab was pouting. He was so upset that he wouldn't eat. Over a vineyard? Seriously?

Ahab, in coveting Naboth's vineyard, broke the tenth commandment. Ahab's childish response to his displeasure of Naboth's refusal of his offer shows his evil, selfish heart. Are we not much different today? How often do we compare ourselves to others and covet what they have? How often do we see something that we think will make us happy and become vexed and sullen if we do not immediately get it? That was the issue with Ahab – he thought that things, such as Naboth's vineyard, were going to satisfy him. Max Lucado, in his book *When God Whispers Your Name*, says that "There is nothing on this earth that can satisfy our deepest longing. We long to see God. The leaves of life are rustling with the rumor that we will

---

[3] Leviticus 25:23 commands God's people that "The land shall not be sold in perpetuity, for the land is mine. For you are strangers and sojourners with me." Numbers 36:7 echoes this command, "The inheritance of the people of Israel shall not be transferred from one tribe to another, for every one of the people of Israel shall hold on to the inheritance of the tribe of his fathers."

[see God] – and we won't be satisfied until we do."[4] Nothing on earth - not health or wealth or even a neighbor's vineyard can satisfy our deepest longings.

Jezebel's Scheme

1 Kings 21:25[5] tells us that Jezebel often incited Ahab to do evil. The story of Naboth's vineyard is no different. In verse 7, Jezebel belittled Ahab, "Since you are not courageous enough to get the vineyard, I will do it for you." She insulted Ahab and basically called him a chicken. She knew very well what she was doing. She callously orchestrated Naboth's murder by forging letters in Ahab's name. She then used Ahab's seal[6] on the letters to make it seem as though he had written them.

The letters instructed the elders and religious leaders to proclaim a fast and set Naboth at the head of the people. They were then to set two worthless men opposite him, who would bring a false charge of blasphemy against him. The people were then to immediately take him out of the city and stone him to death. What a horribly despicable plan! Jezebel's theft of Naboth's vineyard included lies, fraud, forgery, perjury, defamation, and murder. And yet, the religious leaders went along with the scheme and followed her instructions exactly.

Jezebel's sole focus was the death of Naboth. Once that was accomplished, all that remained was taking possession of the vineyard. The charge of blasphemy levied against Naboth was severe. Blasphemy is the act of speaking sacrilegiously about God. Leviticus 24:13-16 lays out the punishment for blasphemy.

---

[4] Max Lucado. *When God Whispers Your Name* (Nashville: Thomas Nelson, 1999), 174.

[5] 1 Kings 21:25, "There was none who sold himself to do what was evil in the sight of the LORD like Ahab, whom Jezebel his wife incited."

[6] A seal was a portable, engraved cylindrical item rolled over wet clay to seal and mark it. Not to be confused with the marine mammal.

Then the LORD spoke to Moses, saying, "Bring out of the camp the one who cursed, and let all who heard him lay their hands on his head, and let all the congregation stone him. And speak to the people of Israel, saying, whoever curses his God shall bear his sin. Whoever blasphemes the name of the LORD shall surely be put to death. All the congregation shall stone him. The sojourner as well as the native, when he blasphemes the name, shall be put to death."

Jezebel knew the punishment for blasphemy was death by stoning. She had Naboth killed by falsely charging him with blasphemy. She used the Israelites' own laws against him.

It is interesting that no one said anything about it. Everybody went along with Jezebel's scheme. No one stood up to her. The level of collusion for her plot was massive - from court officials who gave her access to Ahab's seal, to scribes who wrote the message, to religious leaders and elders of Jezreel, down to the two worthless men who accused Naboth, it seems as though everyone was involved.

We are not told why these individuals went along with the plan. Were they paid off? Were they only doing what they were told? Were they frightened of what would happen to them if they disobeyed the king? The elders in Jezreel were either morally corrupt or were deathly afraid of the evil queen. Nobody could claim to be a spectator. This is injustice, not by a lack of goodness, but by a lack of guts. G.K. Chesterton said, "Men do not disagree on what is evil. They disagree on what evils they will excuse."[7] How often do we see injustice in the world and not do anything about it?

Once Jezebel heard that Naboth was dead, she ordered Ahab to take possession of the vineyard. However, before they could take possession of

---

[7]https://www.azquotes.com/author/2799-Gilbert_K_Chesterton/tag/evil. Accessed August 25, 2024. This quote originally appeared in *"The Illustrated London News" Magazine* October 23, 1909.

the vineyard, Ahab and Jezebel had to take care of one other detail: Naboth's sons. They were in line to receive the land when Naboth died. While 1 Kings 21 does not mention Naboth's sons, 2 Kings 9:26 does: "'As surely as I saw yesterday the blood of Naboth and the blood of his sons—declares the LORD—I will repay you on this plot of ground.' Now therefore take him up and throw him on the plot of ground, in accordance with the word of the LORD." Not only did Ahab and Jezebel have Naboth killed, but they also killed his sons. They just kept on becoming more despicable.

What about Ahab? Where was his guilt in Jezebel's scheme? The purpose of the king was to protect his citizens and to uphold justice. Ahab, by allowing Jezebel to carry out her wicked plan, failed in his role as king. But, by taking possession of the land, Ahab became an active participant and was just as guilty as the murderers. Today, in the modern court system, those who conspire to murder often receive the same sentences as those they hired to do their dirty work. If King Ahab had no knowledge of the scheme up to Naboth's murder, his taking possession of the vineyard made him equally guilty of all that had transpired. Justifiably, Elijah pronounced God's judgment upon the evil masterminds, Ahab and Jezebel.

Aren't we all a bit like Ahab? Have there been times where you disobeyed God's commands, instead, preferring to satisfy your selfish desires?[8] Have there been times you withheld your tithe because you were concerned about your finances? Have you gossiped or lied about someone to make yourself look better? Because I hate being late, there are times that I have disobeyed speed limits in order to arrive somewhere early.[9] We have all likely violated God's laws for personal reasons at one time or another. And, in doing so, we are no better than Ahab.

---

[8] Jesus was the opposite of Ahab. Jesus *obeyed* all God's commands to meet his *selfless* desires.

[9] Yes, you might argue, but the speed limit is not a command of God. But, according to Romans 13:1, each of us must "be subject to the governing authorities. For there is no authority except from God, and those that exist have been instituted by God." Therefore, the laws of the land are there because God instituted our government.

The Outcome

Jezebel's scheme went according to plan and everyone involved must have been pleased with themselves. Ahab would get the vegetable garden next to his palace. Jezebel would no longer have to endure Ahab's pouting and whining. However, just when they seemed to have gotten away with it, Elijah crashed the party. According to verse 19 Elijah said to Ahab, "Thus says the LORD, 'Have you killed and also taken possession... Thus says the LORD: In the place where dogs licked up the blood of Naboth shall dogs lick your own blood.'" Elijah was kind of a killjoy, reminding Ahab that God sees everything, including Ahab's murder of an innocent man.

1 Kings 22:34-38[10] chronicles the death of Ahab. Ahab had been in his chariot, fighting against the Arameans, when he was struck by an arrow. Blood flowed down Ahab's legs to the floor of the chariot. After Ahab died, the chariot was washed out, and dogs licked the blood from his chariot. 2 Kings 9:30-37[11] tells us the story of the death of Jezebel, who

---

[10] 1 Kings 22:34-38, "By chance, a soldier shot an arrow, but he hit Ahab king of Israel between the pieces of his armor. King Ahab said to his chariot driver, 'Turn around and get me out of the battle, because I am hurt!' [35] The battle continued all day. King Ahab was held up in his chariot and faced the Arameans. His blood flowed down to the bottom of the chariot. That evening he died. [36] Near sunset a cry went out through the army of Israel: 'Each man go back to his own city and land.' [37] In that way King Ahab died. His body was carried to Samaria and buried there. [38] The men cleaned Ahab's chariot at a pool in Samaria where prostitutes bathed, and the dogs licked his blood from the chariot. These things happened as the LORD had said they would."

[11] 2 Kings 9:30-37, "When Jehu came to Jezreel, Jezebel heard of it. And she painted her eyes and adorned her head and looked out of the window. [31] And as Jehu entered the gate, she said, 'Is it peace, you Zimri, murderer of your master?' [32] And he lifted up his face to the window and said, 'Who is on my side? Who?' Two or three eunuchs looked out at him. [33] He said, 'Throw her down.' So, they threw her down. And some of her blood spattered on the wall and on the horses, and they trampled on her. [34] Then he went in and ate and drank. And he said, 'See now to this cursed woman and bury her, for she is a king's daughter.' [35] But when they went to bury her, they found no more of her than the skull and the feet and the palms of her hands. [36] When they came back and told him, he said, 'This is the word of the LORD, which he spoke by his servant Elijah the Tishbite: 'In the territory of Jezreel the dogs shall eat the flesh of Jezebel, [37] and the corpse of Jezebel shall be as dung on the face of the field in the territory of Jezreel, so that no one can say, 'This is Jezebel.'"

was thrown from an upper story window, trampled by horses, and her body eaten by dogs. These deaths took place exactly as prophesied by Elijah.

While Elijah announced God's punishment upon Ahab and Jezebel, the timing of God's response seems a little off. While we should be satisfied that Ahab and Jezebel didn't get away with their horrible crime, the timing isn't quite right. As humans, we want them punished immediately.[12] And yet, God allowed them time before their deaths. Why did God do that? Why did he not kill them immediately?

In chapter 2, Joseph's brothers got away with their crimes for years. And even when their sins were revealed, they didn't seem to face any consequences. It was the same with Ahab and Jezebel. Rather than kill them on the spot, God allowed Ahab and Jezebel to enjoy salads from their new garden for some time before Elijah's prophecy of their gruesome deaths was fulfilled.

Ahab's taking of the vineyard underscores the concept that evil seems to prosper in this world. This has been an issue since Old Testament times. Jeremiah 12:1, "Righteous are you, O LORD, when I complain to you; yet I would plead my case before you. Why does the way of the wicked prosper? Why do all who are treacherous thrive?" Psalm 73:3, "For I was envious of the arrogant when I saw the prosperity of the wicked." Ecclesiastes 8:14, "There is a vanity that takes place on earth, that there are righteous people to whom it happens according to the deeds of the wicked, and there are wicked people to whom it happens according to the deeds of the righteous. I said that this also is vanity." When it seems that evil people are prospering, we must remember that God is just, and that evil people will be judged for their actions like Ahab and Jezebel were. God often delays His judgment to allow time for repentance. 2 Peter 3:9 says, "The LORD is not slow to fulfill His promise as some count slowness, but is patient toward you, not wishing that any should perish, but that *all should reach repentance*." (Italics added.)

---

[12] Like they did to Naboth.

God tells us that His timing is not our own.[13] When we see evil and injustice in the world, we may never see the good He works from it. Many times, our only comfort comes from knowing that our suffering does not go unseen by God and He will work it for good. God will not allow injustice to continue forever.

Despite their evil hearts, God was in no hurry to put Ahab and Jezebel to death. He gave them time to repent from their sins and turn to him. God does this with us as well. While we deserve immediate death for our sins, God graciously allows us time so that we may repent and turn to Him. If you have not done so, I encourage you to repent and turn to God with all your heart.

Similarities between Naboth and Jesus Christ

Naboth was a *type* of Christ. According to Hugh Martin, a type is "an event or ordinance in one sphere, analogous to a corresponding event or ordinance in a higher sphere."[14] For example, when the Israelites were in the wilderness, the bronze serpent was lifted up to heal God's chosen people, just as Christ was lifted up on the cross to heal His chosen people. While Naboth is not Jesus Christ, he is "one of the long line of types of Jesus, each representing an aspect of what the Son of God will be in totality."[15] Naboth's story points us forward to the life of Jesus some 850 years later. There are five similarities between Naboth and Jesus.

1. Both were victims of an extensive conspiracy to murder them.
2. Both obeyed the law. According to 1 Kings 21:3, Naboth boldly obeyed the law when he told Ahab, "The LORD forbid that I should give you the inheritance of my fathers." Naboth followed the law for himself. Jesus fulfilled the law for His chosen people.

---

[13] Ecclesiastes 3:1, "For everything there is a season, and a time for every matter under heaven."

[14] Hugh Martin, *Jonah* Geneva Series of Commentaries (Edinburgh: Banner of Truth, 1995), 313.

[15] Jacques Ellul, *The Judgment of Jonah* (Grand Rapids: Eerdmans, 1971), 36-38.

3. Both men were falsely accused of blasphemy. Naboth was accused in 1 Kings 21:13.[16] Jesus was accused in Matthew 26:65, "Then the high priest tore his robes and said, 'He has uttered blasphemy. What further witnesses do we need? You have now heard his blasphemy.'"

4. Both were convicted due to the testimony of two men.[17] According to verse 13, Naboth's conviction occurred when "two worthless men brought a charge against Naboth in the presence of the people, saying, "Naboth cursed God and the king." During Jesus' trial, when searching for witnesses in Matthew 26:60, "they found none, though many false witnesses came forward. At last, two came forward."

5. Neither was protected by an evil king. Ahab failed to stand up to Jezebel, and Herod Antipas failed to stand up his wife Herodias. Because of the inaction of these kings, Naboth and Jesus died.

In this story, God shows His attribute of justice. When we suffer injustice, we must remember God's justice. We need another king; not one who would take, but One who would give. One who would suffer horrifying injustice without inflicting any in return. Witnesses lined up against this King; false charges, legitimized by the government, were pressed against Him, and He was led out of the city to die on a cross in our place. We have a God who promises that He will set all things right. No hidden deed, from forging letters to falsely accusing an innocent man, escapes God's eyes.

---

[16] 1 Kings 21:13, "And the two worthless men came in and sat opposite him. And the worthless men brought a charge against Naboth in the presence of the people, saying, "Naboth cursed God and the king." So, they took him outside the city and stoned him to death with stones."

[17] The law required two witnesses. Deuteronomy 19:15, "A single witness shall not suffice against a person for any crime or for any wrong in connection with any offense that he has committed. Only on the evidence of two witnesses or of three witnesses shall a charge be established."

REVIEW QUESTIONS

1. When Naboth rejected Ahab's offer, Ahab became "vexed and sullen." What things make you vexed and sullen? Is it possible that those things could be an idol?

2. When frustrated, children frequently complain, "that's not fair!" Adults often answer, "Life is not fair." Do you think that God's justice is unfair? Why or why not? Hint: Why is it that we stop complaining about life being unfair when we are adults?

3. What are other Biblical examples where God's punishment was not immediate?

4. Which commandments did Ahab and Jezebel break? What does James 4:1-3 say about it?

5. What are some other similarities between Naboth and Christ?

6. Consider the following verses and comment on how they reflect on how we are to live.

   Psalm 119:36

   1 John 2:15-17

   Proverbs 28:16

Nebuchadnezzar, William Blake. Painting: color monotype with additions in ink and watercolor. 1795-1805. London: Tate Gallery.

8

Nebuchadnezzar

JEREMIAH 25:9

I will send for all the tribes of the north, declares the LORD, and for Nebuchadnezzar the king of Babylon, my servant, and I will bring them against this land and its inhabitants, and against all these surrounding nations. I will devote them to destruction, and make them a horror, a hissing, and an everlasting desolation."

DANIEL 4

King Nebuchadnezzar to all peoples, nations, and languages, that dwell in all the earth: Peace be multiplied to you! [2] *It has seemed good to me to show the signs and wonders that the Most High God has done for me.*

³ How great are His signs,
 how mighty His wonders!
His kingdom is an everlasting kingdom,
 and His dominion endures from generation to generation.
   ⁴ I, Nebuchadnezzar, was at ease in my house and prospering in my palace. ⁵ I saw a dream that made me afraid. As I lay in bed the fancies and the visions of my head alarmed me. ⁶ So I made a decree that all the wise men of Babylon should be brought before me, that they might make known to me the interpretation of the dream. ⁷ Then the magicians, the enchanters, the Chaldeans, and the astrologers came in, and I told them the dream, but they could not make known to me its interpretation. ⁸ At last Daniel came in before me—he who was named Belteshazzar after the name of my god, and in whom is the spirit of the holy gods—and I told him the dream, saying, ⁹ "O Belteshazzar, chief of the magicians, because I know that the spirit of the holy gods is in you and that no mystery is too difficult for you, tell me the visions of my dream that I saw and their interpretation. ¹⁰ The visions of my head as I lay in bed were these: I saw, and behold, a tree in the midst of the earth, and its height was great. ¹¹ The tree grew and became strong, and its top reached to heaven, and it was visible to the end of the whole earth. ¹² Its leaves were beautiful and its fruit abundant, and in it was food for all. The beasts of the field found shade under it, and the birds of the heavens lived in its branches, and all flesh was fed from it.
   ¹³ "I saw in the visions of my head as I lay in bed, and behold, a watcher, a holy one, came down from heaven. ¹⁴ He proclaimed aloud and said thus: 'Chop down the tree and lop off its branches, strip off its leaves and scatter its fruit. Let the beasts flee from under it and the birds from its branches. ¹⁵ But leave the stump of its roots in the earth, bound with a band of iron and bronze, amid the tender grass of the field. Let him be wet with the dew of heaven. Let his portion be with the beasts in the grass of the earth. ¹⁶ Let his mind be changed from a man's and let a beast's mind be given to him; and let seven periods of time pass over him. ¹⁷ The sentence is by the decree of the watchers, the decision by the word of the holy ones,

to the end that the living may know that the Most High rules the kingdom of men and gives it to whom he will and sets over it the lowliest of men.' [18] This dream I, King Nebuchadnezzar, saw. And you, O Belteshazzar, tell me the interpretation, because all the wise men of my kingdom are not able to make known to me the interpretation, but you are able, for the spirit of the holy gods is in you."

[19] Then Daniel, whose name was Belteshazzar, was dismayed for a while, and his thoughts alarmed him. The king answered and said, "Belteshazzar, let not the dream or the interpretation alarm you." Belteshazzar answered and said, "My lord, may the dream be for those who hate you and its interpretation for your enemies! [20] The tree you saw, which grew and became strong, so that its top reached to heaven, and it was visible to the end of the whole earth, [21] whose leaves were beautiful and its fruit abundant, and in which was food for all, under which beasts of the field found shade, and in whose branches the birds of the heavens lived— [22] it is you, O king, who have grown and become strong. Your greatness has grown and reaches to heaven, and your dominion to the ends of the earth. [23] And because the king saw a watcher, a holy one, coming down from heaven and saying, 'Chop down the tree and destroy it, but leave the stump of its roots in the earth, bound with a band of iron and bronze, in the tender grass of the field, and let him be wet with the dew of heaven, and let his portion be with the beasts of the field, till seven periods of time pass over him,' [24] this is the interpretation, O king: It is a decree of the Most High, which has come upon my lord the king, [25] that you shall be driven from among men, and your dwelling shall be with the beasts of the field. You shall be made to eat grass like an ox, and you shall be wet with the dew of heaven, and seven periods of time shall pass over you, till you know that the Most High rules the kingdom of men and gives it to whom He will. [26] And as it was commanded to leave the stump of the roots of the tree, your kingdom shall be confirmed for you from the time that you know that Heaven rules. [27] Therefore, O king, let my counsel be acceptable to you: break off your sins by practicing righteousness, and

your iniquities by showing mercy to the oppressed, that there may perhaps be a lengthening of your prosperity."

[28] All this came upon King Nebuchadnezzar. [29] At the end of twelve months he was walking on the roof of the royal palace of Babylon, [30] and the king answered and said, "Is not this great Babylon, which I have built by my mighty power as a royal residence and for the glory of my majesty?" [31] While the words were still in the king's mouth, there fell a voice from heaven, "O King Nebuchadnezzar, to you it is spoken: The kingdom has departed from you, [32] and you shall be driven from among men, and your dwelling shall be with the beasts of the field. And you shall be made to eat grass like an ox, and seven periods of time shall pass over you, until you know that the Most High rules the kingdom of men and gives it to whom He will." [33] Immediately the word was fulfilled against Nebuchadnezzar. He was driven from among men and ate grass like an ox, and his body was wet with the dew of heaven till his hair grew as long as eagles' feathers, and his nails were like birds' claws.

[34] At the end of the days I, Nebuchadnezzar, lifted my eyes to heaven, and my reason returned to me, and I blessed the Most High, and praised and honored Him who lives forever, for His dominion is an everlasting dominion, and His kingdom endures from generation to generation; [35] all the inhabitants of the earth are accounted as nothing, and He does according to His will among the host of heaven and among the inhabitants of the earth; and none can stay His hand or say to Him, "What have you done?"

[36] At the same time my reason returned to me, and for the glory of my kingdom, my majesty and splendor returned to me. My counselors and my lords sought me, and I was established in my kingdom, and still more greatness was added to me. [37] Now I, Nebuchadnezzar, praise and extol and honor the King of heaven, for all His works are right and His ways are just; and those who walk in pride He is able to humble.

THROUGHOUT OLD TESTAMENT ISRAEL, NO name has struck more fear into the hearts of the Hebrews than Nebuchadnezzar. Nebuchadnezzar was the longest reigning king of Babylon, ruling from 605 to 562 B.C. The prophet Jeremiah described Nebuchadnezzar as "God's servant."[1] In the Old Testament prophetic books, Nebuchadnezzar was frequently used by God to brutally punish Israel for their sins. The Israelites, on the other hand, referred to Nebuchadnezzar at the "destroyer of nations."[2] According to Jeremiah 21:7,[3] Nebuchadnezzar and his army would "strike them down with the edge of the sword. He shall not pity them or spare them or have compassion."

Did you know?

According to the Talmud, the Jewish code of civil and ceremonial law, Nebuchadnezzar was a dwarf. Naturally, people under-estimated him. However, he had immense courage. Rumor has it that he trained a lion and rode it bareback around his palace.

The degree of destruction which Nebuchadnezzar's army delivered to enemy nations was similar to a "scorched earth" policy and was frequently aimed at stopping an Egyptian presence in the area. The sworn enemy of Babylon was Pharaoh Necho II. Wars fought in the ancient Near East at the time were often done so to remove Egyptian influence in the region.

---

[1] Jeremiah 25:9.

[2] Jeremiah 4:7, "A lion has gone up from his thicket, a *destroyer of nations* has set out; he has gone out from his place to make your land a waste; your cities will be ruins without inhabitant." (Italics added.)

[3] Jeremiah 21:7, "Afterward, declares the LORD, I will give Zedekiah king of Judah and his servants and the people in this city who survive the pestilence, sword, and famine into the hand of Nebuchadnezzar king of Babylon and into the hand of their enemies, into the hand of those who seek their lives. He shall strike them down with the edge of the sword. He shall not pity them or spare them or have compassion."

Nebuchadnezzar attempted to invade Egypt but failed. As a result, many of the cities under Babylonian control rebelled, only to be crushed by the Babylonian army again. One such rebel was the Jewish king, Zedekiah, who was caught attempting to flee after rebelling against Babylon. According to 2 Kings 25:5-7,[4] Nebuchadnezzar made an example out of him. Zedekiah was taken to Riblah in northern Syria, where he watched his sons' executions before having his eyes gouged out. The last thing Zedekiah saw was the death of his sons. This was typically the way the Babylonian army, under the command of Nebuchadnezzar, treated their enemies.

Nebuchadnezzar's army was violent and ruthless. His military policy was population control via terror. In lands that his army captured, Nebuchadnezzar appointed satraps[5] who were loyal to him. As a general rule, he did not relocate the populations that he captured.[6] They were, however, oppressed into submission. In 597 BC, he invaded Judah, captured Jerusalem, and deposed its king, Jehoiachin. After an 18-month siege, Jerusalem was captured in 587 BC. Thousands of Jews were taken captive to Babylon and Solomon's Temple was burned to the ground. By 572, Nebuchadnezzar controlled all of Babylonia, Assyria, Phoenicia, Israel, Philistia, northern Arabia, parts of Asia Minor, and all the trade routes in between.

Naturally, Nebuchadnezzar was quite proud of his military conquests. After all, it was he who conquered a huge chunk of the Ancient Near East. One cannot conquer that much territory without having an ego. A military leader without some semblance of self-confidence would be seen as weak by his enemies. And Nebuchadnezzar did not want to appear weak.

---

[4] 2 Kings 25:5-7, "But the army of the Chaldeans pursued the king and overtook him in the plains of Jericho, and all his army was scattered from him. [6] Then they captured the king and brought him up to the king of Babylon at Riblah, and they passed sentence on him. [7] They slaughtered the sons of Zedekiah before his eyes and put out the eyes of Zedekiah and bound him in chains and took him to Babylon."

[5] A satrap was a puppet-governor of a province in ancient Persia.

[6] Exceptions were made for royalty and healthy young men.

As a city planner, Nebuchadnezzar was a spectacular builder. Using the spoils of war to finance his building projects, he rebuilt cities on a lavish scale. He turned the capital city of Babylon into the immense and beautiful city of legend. Babylon boasted a population of over 200,000. The city of Babylon covered more than four square miles, surrounded by moats and a double circuit of walls. The Euphrates River flowed through the city's center, spanned by a beautiful stone bridge. At the center of the city was a huge temple to Marduk, the Babylonian god of weather and agriculture. Nebuchadnezzar allegedly built the Hanging Gardens of Babylon[7] to cheer up his wife, Amytis, who was homesick for her mountainous home.

Nebuchadnezzar rebuilt the palace in Babylon and refurnished the city's processional street. He built the Ishtar Gate which opened up into the processional street, which led into the city. The Ishtar Gate was a double gate with a smaller frontal gate and a larger posterior section. The walls of the gate were finished with lapis lazuli[8] glazed blue bricks. The Ishtar Gate is decorated with images of three animals: lions, bulls, and dragons, each one representing a different Babylonian god. The gate was 15 meters tall and the foundation extended another 15 meters into the ground.[9]

Nebuchadnezzar had a lot to be proud of, in his military prowess and his work as a builder. His accomplishments were unrivaled in his lifetime. But, as a result, Nebuchadnezzar was prideful. In Daniel 4:30, he boasts, "Is not this great Babylon, which *I have built by my mighty power* as a royal residence and *for the glory of my majesty*?" (Italics added.)

---

[7] There are several views on the existence of the Hanging Gardens. Hellenistic culture lists them as one of the original seven wonders of the world. However, Herodotus, in his volume, *Histories*, described Babylon in detail, but never mentioned the Hanging Gardens. Other archaeologists hypothesize that the Hanging Gardens were located in Nineveh rather than Babylon.

[8] Lapis lazuli is a semi-precious stone known for its deep blue color. Anyone who plays Minecraft should know this.

[9] The gate is now housed in the Pergamon Museum in Berlin.

Nebuchadnezzar's Prior Exposure to God

Nebuchadnezzar, throughout his life, was exposed to God in a variety of settings. In Daniel 1, after conquering the land of Judah, Nebuchadnezzar had the Jewish royal family, nobles, and healthy youth relocated to Babylon. This included Daniel, Shadrach, Meshach, and Abednego. While in Nebuchadnezzar's service, the four youth grew physically and mentally, eventually becoming wiser than the king's advisors. In Daniel 2, Nebuchadnezzar had a dream and wanted it to be interpreted. None of his wise men could do so except Daniel, who glorified God by explaining the dream to him. Nebuchadnezzar's response to Daniel's interpretation acknowledged God and praised Him, "Truly, your God is God of gods and LORD of kings, and a revealer of mysteries, for you have been able to reveal this mystery." (Daniel 2:47)

In Daniel 3, Nebuchadnezzar built a gold statue and commanded the people to bow down to it. Shadrach, Meshach, and Abednego refused to do so, and were thrown in the fiery furnace as punishment. While they were in the furnace, a fourth figure stood with them. When the men exited the furnace without being burned at all, Nebuchadnezzar exclaimed, "Blessed be the God of Shadrach, Meshach, and Abednego, who has sent His angel and delivered His servants, who trusted in Him, and set aside the king's command, and yielded up their bodies rather than serve and worship any god except their own God. Therefore, I make a decree: Any people, nation, or language that speaks anything against the God of Shadrach, Meshach, and Abednego shall be torn limb from limb, and their houses laid in ruins, for there is no other god who is able to rescue in this way."[10] God had revealed himself to Nebuchadnezzar repeatedly through the devotion and actions of his servants and by using miracles, and yet Nebuchadnezzar had not worshiped the LORD. He was still too proud. Pride *almost* became Nebuchadnezzar's downfall.

---

[10] Daniel 3:28-29

The Letter
Daniel 4:1-3 says,

> King Nebuchadnezzar to all peoples, nations, and languages that dwell in all the earth: Peace be multiplied to you! [2] It has seemed good to me to show the signs and wonders that the Most High God has done for me. [3] How great are His signs, how mighty His wonders! His kingdom is an everlasting kingdom, and His dominion endures from generation to generation.

In Ancient Near Eastern letters, the author's name went at the top of the letter, followed by the recipients' names, and then the purpose of the letter. In his letter, King Nebuchadnezzar wrote to all peoples, nations, and languages on earth. He then explained, "It has seemed good to me to show the signs and wonders that the Most High God has done for me." In verse 3, Nebuchadnezzar wrote a doxology.[11] The chief god of Babylon was Marduk. Nebuchadnezzar had previously built an elaborate temple to Marduk in the center of the city. Now, he sent a letter to all of his people, praising the "Most High God" as an offering of thanks and to tell of all the signs and wonders God had done for him. What happened to change who he worshiped? How did this change in Nebuchadnezzar's life come about?

The Dream
In Daniel 4, Nebuchadnezzar had another dream. As with his dream of the statue, his wise men could not recount the dream or interpret it for him. Again, Nebuchadnezzar called for Daniel. In Daniel 4:4-18, Daniel correctly recounted the dream and provided the interpretation of it. He told King Nebuchadnezzar that he was the tree and that God would cut him down and drive him from his kingdom. He would be like a beast of the

---

[11] A doxology is an expression of thanks to God.

field and eat grass like an ox for seven years,[12] but his kingdom would be restored to him.[13]

The purpose of this divine punishment was then proclaimed: "The sentence is by the decree of the watchers, the decision by the word of the holy ones, to the end that the living may know that the Most High rules the kingdom of men and gives it to whom He will and sets over it the lowliest of men." God was going to punish Nebuchadnezzar so that he and those around him would know that the LORD rules over the kingdom of men.

The Punishment

Nebuchadnezzar did not acknowledge God's dominion and providence in his military victories and building projects. So, a little later in Daniel 4, Nebuchadnezzar received his punishment. God waited twelve months before punishing Nebuchadnezzar. Why? By waiting, God allowed him the opportunity to repent. The punishment did not begin until Nebuchadnezzar fell back into his despicable pattern of pride. In verse 30, he boasts, "Is not this great Babylon, which *I have built by my mighty power* as a royal residence and for *the glory of my majesty*?" (Italics added.) As a result, God punished Nebuchadnezzar for seven years.[14]

---

[12] The Hebrew word used in Daniel 4:25 and 4:32 is '*iddānîn*, which is a noun meaning a set time, specifically one year. However, it can also mean a period of time or a season.

[13] Daniel 4:24-26, "This is the interpretation, O king: It is a decree of the Most High, which has come upon my lord the king, [25] that you shall be driven from among men, and your dwelling shall be with the beasts of the field. You shall be made to eat grass like an ox, and you shall be wet with the dew of heaven, and seven periods of time shall pass over you, till you know that the Most High rules the kingdom of men and gives it to whom he will. [26] And as it was commanded to leave the stump of the roots of the tree, your kingdom shall be confirmed for you from the time that you know that Heaven rules."

[14] Daniel 4:31-32, "While the words were still in the king's mouth, there fell a voice from heaven, 'O King Nebuchadnezzar, to you it is spoken: The kingdom has departed from you. and you shall be driven from among men, and your dwelling shall be with the beasts of the field. And you shall be made to eat grass like an ox, and seven periods of time shall pass over you, until you know that the Most High rules the kingdom of men and gives it to whom He will.'"

God's judgment of Nebuchadnezzar involved complete and utter humiliation.[15] Nebuchadnezzar went from being human to being sub-human.[16] Nebuchadnezzar is the first recorded case of *boanthropy*, where a person believes themself to be an ox or cow and attempts to live and behave accordingly. Human stomachs aren't designed to digest grass, so the fact that Nebuchadnezzar survived in his bovine state is miraculous. God could have easily left Nebuchadnezzar to die in the field with a mouthful of rye grass, but He didn't. God not only altered his organs and appearance but He also saw to it that the king didn't become food for wild animals during this period. We should be careful not to miss all that God did to save Nebuchadnezzar. The Great Shepherd protected His sheep, or in this case, His ox.

Our text does not dwell on Nebuchadnezzar's time as an ox. In the very next verse,[17] God showed mercy to Nebuchadnezzar by granting him an opportunity to repent. The phrase, "lifted my eyes to heaven" is another way of saying "looking to God." Once Nebuchadnezzar repented, his sanity was restored and he began to praise God. Nebuchadnezzar spent the final years of his life praising the one true God. He returned to his position as king and ruled an additional seven years. Says Alex Kirk, "Nebuchadnezzar's experience as a beast changed his perspective toward the divine."[18] Nebuchadnezzar, due to his time as an ox, now finally understood his complete dependence on God.

---

[15] Daniel 4:33, "Immediately the word was fulfilled against Nebuchadnezzar. He was driven from among men and ate grass like an ox, and his body was wet with the dew of heaven till his hair grew as long as eagles' feathers, and his nails were like birds' claws."

[16] There are some who maintain that the story of Nebuchadnezzar's change serves as the inspiration behind the fairy tale of *Beauty and the Beast*. However, Nebuchadnezzar's story was no fairy tale.

[17] Daniel 4:34, "At the end of the days I, Nebuchadnezzar, lifted my eyes to heaven, and my reason returned to me, and I blessed the Most High, and praised and honored Him who lives forever, for His dominion is an everlasting dominion, and His kingdom endures from generation to generation."

[18] https://www.thegospelcoalition.org/article/understanding-daniel-4/ Accessed June 14, 2024.

From Pride to Humility

Nebuchadnezzar's transformation from prideful monarch to beast of the field to worshiper of the Most High God is an odd one indeed. Nebuchadnezzar's sin was not just that he was proud; it's that he thought he didn't need God. Sinful pride is an attitude of independence from God. Those who believe that they don't need God live as though they brought themselves to their current status in life. Nebuchadnezzar thought he was responsible for the conquered territories and his majestic city of Babylon when it was God who allowed the victories and the city to be built. Nebuchadnezzar thought that he had no need for God. However, Scripture repeatedly warns against sinful pride and tells us to humble ourselves.

1. Proverbs 11:2 says, "When pride comes, then comes disgrace, but with the humble is wisdom."
2. Proverbs 16:18 tells us, "Pride goes before destruction, and a haughty spirit before a fall."
3. Luke 14:11, "For everyone who exalts himself will be humbled, and he who humbles himself will be exalted."
4. James 4:10 says, "Humble yourselves before the Lord, and he will exalt you."

These are just a few examples of the hundreds of times that Scripture discusses pride. Many of them describe how God detests the proud, stands against them, and will bring them low. Why is pride such a big deal? Why did Nebuchadnezzar have to be punished so harshly for his pride? Indeed, he was guilty of many sins that God could have punished him for including murder and genocide. In verse 27 Daniel encouraged him to "break from his sins and iniquities by practicing righteousness and showing mercy to the oppressed."[19] Daniel may not have thought that Nebuchadnezzar giving up his pride was the top priority. *But God did.* Why?

---

[19] The above quote is my paraphrase from the Hebrew text. Daniel 4:27 (ESV) reads, "Therefore, O king, let my counsel be acceptable to you: break off your sins by practicing righteousness, and your iniquities by showing mercy to the oppressed, that there may perhaps be a lengthening of your prosperity."

The problem with pride is that it places the self at the center of our worship. If we are residing on the throne of our hearts, there is no room for God. If we think we don't need God, we very quickly begin to live as if God does not matter. In our hearts, God becomes irrelevant. God's view of man's futile efforts to exalt himself are revealed by the Bible's staunch condemnation of pride and promises that it will result in being brought low. The more we try to lift ourselves up, the more God will humble us. We cannot worship God when we worship ourselves. And we cannot recognize our need for a savior if we do not see how low we are. And that salvation freely applied to us by grace cannot be earned by our works or accomplishments.

Pride and Salvation

The concept of salvation by grace runs contrary to pride. Since man is unable to save himself by his own achievements, he must rely upon another for salvation. We are saved, not due to anything we have done, but by the righteousness of God's Son and what He has done. Ephesians 2:8-9 tells us, "For by grace you have been saved through faith. And this is not your own doing; it is the gift of God, not a result of works, so that no one may boast." In a very tongue-in-cheek statement, D.L. Moody once said, "I'm glad we are saved by grace and not by good works. Because I don't want to sit in heaven and listen to everybody brag for eternity on how they got there."[20] Since those who are saved have been saved by grace, we have nothing to be proud about. Our salvation is a gift from God. We, like Nebuchadnezzar, are fully dependent upon Him for our every need – especially our salvation. Sinful pride causes us to ignore God. Therefore, we are to repent of that sinful pride and return to Him who placed us where we are.

---

[20] https://moodycenter.org/the-quotable-moody-d-l-moody-quotes/ Accessed January 29, 2025.

Afterthought

In a way, Nebuchadnezzar is a forerunner to Christ. According to Daniel 2:37,[21] Nebuchadnezzar was the king of kings.[22] At the height of his glory and power, he was humbled by becoming a beast of burden. Jesus Christ, the King of kings, left His glory and power and humbled himself to become a human, much less, a servant.[23] Nebuchadnezzar became a wild animal, but Jesus became the sacrificial lamb. Says Alex Kirk, "This move from very God to humble human parallels Nebuchadnezzar's descent from great king to lowly beast... Jesus' humility is the prelude to His exaltation over heaven and earth, while Nebuchadnezzar's humility is the prelude to the praising the King of heaven."[24]

Nebuchadnezzar's humility came against his will. Jesus' humility was a voluntary choice on our behalf. God did not allow Christ's death to be the end. He was restored to His throne and reigns there still.

---

[21] Daniel 2:37, "You, O king, the king of kings, to whom the God of heaven has given the kingdom, the power, and the might, and the glory."

[22] This was a title frequently claimed by kings of the Babylonian and Assyrian empires.

[23] Philippians 2:6-7 speaks of Jesus, "who, though He was in the form of God, did not count equality with God a thing to be grasped, [7] but emptied Himself, by taking the form of a servant, being born in the likeness of men."

[24] https://www.thegospelcoalition.org/article/understanding-daniel-4/ Accessed June 14, 2024.

REVIEW QUESTIONS

1. Nebuchadnezzar experienced real repentance which was stated to be one of the things that set the villains apart from the heroes of the faith. Why do you think the author chose to include him?

2. Pride and boasting are not always sinful. When is this the case?

3. Nebuchadnezzar had good reason to be proud, but God was deeply offended by his sinful pride. Are there some sins that seem less offensive to us than they are to God?

4. Failure to rely on God is at the core of sinful pride. What idol worship is involved in sinful pride?

5. Nebuchadnezzar didn't turn to God until he was stripped of his pride and brought to the lowest point in his life. Who are other Biblical

characters that needed to be stripped of pride before they could accomplish God's work?

6. Nebuchadnezzar's experience as a beast changed his perspective toward the divine. In Daniel 4:34-35, Nebuchadnezzar proclaimed truths about God that he had learned. Describe how his statements reflected his newfound beliefs.

7. Nebuchadnezzar is a forerunner to Jesus Christ. Who are some other forerunners to Christ?

8. Consider the following verses and comment on how they reflect on how we are to live.

    Isaiah 55:8-9

    Matthew 23:1-12, 27-28

    Romans 12:3

Massacre of the Innocents, Peter Paul Rubens. Painting: oil on canvas, 1611-1612. Toronto: Art Gallery of Ontario.

9

Herod the Great

*　　　　　　　　　*

MATTHEW 2:1-21

Now after Jesus was born in Bethlehem of Judea in the days of Herod the king, behold, wise men from the east came to Jerusalem, ² saying, "Where is He who has been born King of the Jews? For we saw His star when it rose and have come to worship Him." ³ When Herod the king heard this, he was troubled, and all Jerusalem with him; ⁴ and assembling all the chief priests and scribes of the people, he inquired of them where the Christ was to be born. ⁵ They told him, "In Bethlehem of Judea, for so it is written by the prophet:

⁶ "'And you, O Bethlehem, in the land of Judah,
are by no means least among the rulers of Judah;
for from you shall come a ruler
who will shepherd my people Israel.'"

⁷ Then Herod summoned the wise men secretly and ascertained from them what time the star had appeared. ⁸ And he sent them to Bethlehem, saying, "Go and search diligently for the child, and when you have found Him, bring me word, that I too may come and worship Him." ⁹ After listening to the king, they went on their way. And behold, the star that they had seen when it rose went before them until it came to rest over the place where the child was. ¹⁰ When they saw the star, they rejoiced exceedingly with great joy. ¹¹ And going into the house, they saw the child with Mary His mother, and they fell down and worshiped Him. Then, opening their treasures, they offered Him gifts, gold and frankincense and myrrh. ¹² And being warned in a dream not to return to Herod, they departed to their own country by another way.

¹³ Now when they had departed, behold, an angel of the LORD appeared to Joseph in a dream and said, "Rise, take the child and His mother, and flee to Egypt, and remain there until I tell you, for Herod is about to search for the child, to destroy Him." ¹⁴ And he rose and took the child and His mother by night and departed to Egypt ¹⁵ and remained there until the death of Herod. This was to fulfill what the LORD had spoken by the prophet, "Out of Egypt I called my Son."

¹⁶ Then Herod, when he saw that he had been tricked by the wise men, became furious, and he sent and killed all the male children in Bethlehem and in all that region who were two years old or under, according to the time that he had ascertained from the wise men. ¹⁷ Then was fulfilled what was spoken by the prophet Jeremiah:

[18] "A voice was heard in Ramah,
weeping and loud lamentation,
Rachel weeping for her children;
she refused to be comforted, because they are no more."

[19] But when Herod died, behold, an angel of the LORD appeared in a dream to Joseph in Egypt, [20] saying, "Rise, take the child and His mother and go to the land of Israel, for those who sought the child's life are dead." [21] And he rose and took the child and His mother and went to the land of Israel.

WHILE HEROD IS PRIMARILY KNOWN in Christian circles for ordering the massacre of the baby boys of Bethlehem, he was actually much worse than that. Herod, throughout his life, displayed a general disregard for the sanctity of human life. The death of Bethlehem's boys is just a drop in the bucket of the many slaughtered by this evil king.

Herod I, also known as Herod the Great, was the Roman king of Judea from 37 BC to 4 BC. He is known for his enormous building projects, including the expansion of the Second Temple in Jerusalem (Herod's Temple), the construction of the port at Caesarea, the desert fortress at Masada,[1] and Herodium (a palace-fortress and small town located 12 miles south of Jerusalem).

---

[1] In 73 AD, 960 Jewish rebels were besieged by Roman forces at Masada. The Jews ultimately committed mass suicide to avoid being taken by the Romans. Ironically, 70 years after his reign, Herod's legacy of death continued.

When Herod was a boy, his father, Antipater, was the chief minister of Judea. He was an Idumean, a descendant of Esau (Edom).[2] Antipater was an astute politician, joining whichever side would benefit him the most. He walked the line between Rome and the Jewish people, for if he openly supported Rome, the Jews would hate him. However, if he supported the Jews, he would lose his position with Rome. Herod observed his father's precarious political position for years, until his father was poisoned to death by the Jews. Herod witnessed first-hand the insecurity of political power. When the time availed him, Herod married a Hasmonean[3] princess and endeared himself to Rome.[4] The Roman Senate appointed Herod to be their vassal king in Judea.[5] Along with the position, Herod inherited the insecurity that accompanied it. This insecurity impacted every area of his life.

Herod achieved great success in his position as a vassal king. However, Herod was king in title alone. His entire administration deferred to Rome. Like his father, Herod had to walk the fine line between the Jews and the Romans. But, as long as he kept the peace between Rome and Judea, he kept his position of power.

Herod, the Family Man

Herod was terribly insecure. Throughout his 33-year reign, he was paranoid about the security of his position of authority. He was a power-hungry king who never thought twice about eliminating any threat to his throne. In the ancient Near East, being related to a ruling monarch was

---

[2] The Jewish ruling class despised Herod as king because he was not a descendant of Jacob. To rectify this, Herod had all his family's genealogical records destroyed so no one could prove his lineage.

[3] The Hasmoneans were a Jewish ruling family who ruled Judea until the beginning of Herod the Great's reign. By marrying a Hasmonean princess, Herod was politically aligning himself in order to take power.

[4] Endearing himself to Rome was quite easy for Herod since his father and Caesar Augustus had a great relationship.

[5] A vassal king is one who must obey another. The Romans installed vassal kings rather than send a governor to oversee an area. Pilate was technically a prefect; therefore, his responsibility was the Roman military presence in Judea.

frequently a liability. Rulers often killed or exiled their families to eliminate threats to the throne. But even by those standards, Herod was ruthless in his treatment of family. Early in his reign, Herod had his brother Aristobulus III appointed as high priest so that the Jews couldn't make him king in Herod's place. Herod then invited him to a party at his palace in Jericho. Herod allowed his brother to swim for a bit and then had him drowned.

During his lifetime, Herod married ten wives and had six children. When he became king, he banished his first wife, Doris, and their son, Antipater. He then married Miriamne, a Hasmonean Maccabean princess. She was his favorite wife of the ten, however, he executed her along with their two sons, Alexander and Aristobulus. Mariamne's mother and brother were also executed when he suspected them of plotting against him. He then brought his first wife, Doris, and their son, Antipater, back to court. Five days before his own death, he killed Antipater because Antipater mistakenly thought his father was dead. Three of his sons, two of his wives, his brother, his mother-in-law, brother-in-law, uncles, cousins, and countless others met the same fate when they, too, fell victim to Herod's vast insecurity regarding conspiracies, real or imagined.

> "It would be better to be Herod's pig than Herod's son."
>
> CAESAR AUGUSTUS

The quote from Caesar Augustus shows that his reputation for murdering family members was well known. Herod would keep the kosher laws and not kill swine, but he had no problem taking human lives, even those of his own family. However, Herod didn't limit the bloodshed to family alone. He killed plenty of others in his endless quest for political security. After all, if a man is willing to murder his own sons, why wouldn't he be willing to murder other people's sons? The Jewish historian Josephus recorded that when Herod came to power, he killed all but one of the members of the Sanhedrin, the Jewish ruling council.[6] According to Josephus, in 30 BC, Herod had John Hyrcanus II strangled for being involved in a suspected plot to take Herod's throne from him.[7] Later, he had 45 principal men of the Hasmonean priesthood executed. He also killed Antigonus, who was the last surviving Hasmonean king of Judea. Another time, five Judean cities rebelled against him. He killed all 2,000 survivors of those cities. In 7 BC, he had 300 of his top military leaders executed.[8] Herod tolerated no opposition. He appeared in the gospel of Matthew as the ruler of Judea, who ordered the massacre of the male children in Bethlehem at the time of the birth of Jesus. As a final act of vengeance against his subjects, he rounded up leading Jews and commanded that at his death, they should be executed. He reasoned that if there was no mourning *for him*, at least there would be mourning *at his death*. When he died, however, the order was overruled, and the prisoners were released. Herod's insecurities led to the death of countless people. But his paranoia and brutality were most famously displayed in the despicable massacre of the innocents, as found Matthew 2:1-12.

That story took place when Herod had been ruling for some 30+ years and was nearing the end of his reign. Caesar Augustus had just declared a census, in which everyone in a Roman occupied land had to return to their hometown in order to register.[9] Mary and Joseph left the village of Nazareth in Northern Israel to register for the Roman census in their family's original home of Bethlehem in the south. While in Bethlehem, Mary gave birth to Jesus Christ, the newborn "King of the Jews."

---

[6]   https://www.encyclopedia.com/religion/encyclopedias-almanacs-transcripts-and-maps /herod-i Accessed August 29, 2023.

[7] Flavius Josephus, *The Complete Works*, Antiquities, 15:173-178 (Nashville: Thomas Nelson, 1998), 490.

[8] Josephus, 539.

[9] Luke 2:1, "In those days a decree went out from Caesar Augustus that all the world should be registered."

Visitors from the East

Unbeknownst to everyone at the time, magi from Persia began a long journey westward looking for this newborn King of the Jews. These Asian scholars of religion, magic, wisdom, and astrology had seen a star announcing the birth of a king. The wise men arrived at Herod's palace and asked to see the newborn King of the Jews.[10] Why stop at the palace? As foreigners, they reasonably assumed that's where a newborn king would be found. Verse 3 says that "when Herod the king heard this, he was troubled, and all Jerusalem with him." All of Jerusalem was troubled because of the king's wrath and ruthless methods when he perceived a threat. The wise men brought good news, but it bothered Herod to learn that there was a rival to his throne. Since he was not an expert in the Scriptures, Herod called in the chief priests and religious scholars, who referred him to Micah 5:2: "As for you, Bethlehem of Ephrathah... one who is to be ruler in Israel on my behalf will come out from you."

Never short on strategy when perceiving a threat, Herod sent for the magi and feigned interest in their quest. He told the magi to find this newborn king and check back with him so he might join them in worship and celebration.[11] The magi heeded the Jewish scholars' direction and found Joseph, Mary, and Jesus in the house where they were living, as the star directed. They offered gifts fit for royalty: gold, frankincense, and myrrh. Providentially, these gifts would allow Joseph to pay the expenses incurred in journeying to the land of Egypt and in supporting his family there till he could return to his home and his business.

The contrast in the story of Herod and the wise men is stark: a group of foreign pilgrims bow before the promised Messiah from God, while the king of the Jews plots to murder Him. Charles Spurgeon says, "Those far

---

[10] Matthew 2:2, "Where is He who has been born King of the Jews? For we saw His star when it rose and have come to worship Him."

[11] Matthew 2:7-8, "Then Herod summoned the wise men secretly and ascertained from them what time the star had appeared. [8] And he sent them to Bethlehem, saying, 'Go and search diligently for the child, and when you have found Him, bring me word, that I too may come and worship Him.'"

away drew near. Those near, were far away."[12] The magi were warned in a dream not to return to Herod, and they quietly slipped away on a different route home.[13] Herod, when he realized what had occurred, was incensed. He was, once again, anxious about his throne.

Herod's Despicable Response

When he realized that the Magi had tricked him, Herod's anger was predictably excessive and violent. Verse 16 says that "He sent and killed all the male children in Bethlehem and in all that region who were two years old or under, according to the time that he had ascertained from the wise men." He executed all boys born in Bethlehem under two years of age[14] to ensure he killed the child king, Jesus.

While it seems over the top at first, Herod's order of mass infanticide was typical for him.[15] He had made it his practice to kill any perceived competition for his throne. Baby boys in the small town of Bethlehem were no big deal for Herod.

The Scope of Herod's Infanticide

How many babies did Herod kill to alleviate the stress of maintaining his throne? Was it on the same scale as that of Pharaoh killing the Israelite boys? Before we can answer those questions, we must consider the size of Bethlehem. From the time of Ruth and Naomi, Bethlehem had always been

---

[12] Charles H. Spurgeon. "The Far-Off, Near; The Near, Far Off." Sermon at Metropolitan Tabernacle, London, August 11, 1889.

[13] Matthew 2:12, "And being warned in a dream not to return to Herod, they departed to their own country by another way."

[14] A census could take a long time, and it seems that two years had passed since Jesus was born. This tells us the magi had journeyed for two years to find Jesus. It also explains why they visited Jesus in a house, and not the stable as the shepherds have done.

[15] Matthew 2:16-18, "Then Herod, when he saw that he had been tricked by the wise men, became furious, and he sent and killed all the male children in Bethlehem and in all that region who were two years old or under, according to the time that he had ascertained from the wise men.[17] Then was fulfilled what was spoken by the prophet Jeremiah:[18] 'A voice was heard in Ramah, weeping and loud lamentation, Rachel weeping for her children; she refused to be comforted, because they are no more.'"

Psychoanalyzing Herod the Great

According to a group of Biblical scholars, psychologists, and psychiatrists, Herod went through repeated cycles in his life. He would hear rumors of someone trying to usurp his throne, kill them, plummet into depression, and bring himself out of depression with one of his massive building projects. He would then hear of someone else attempting to take his throne, and the cycle would repeat. Psychiatrists have historically diagnosed him with paranoid personality disorder.

a small town. According to Professor William F. Albright, Bethlehem could have had as few as 300 citizens at the time of Christ.[16] Dr. Stephen J. Pfann places the population between 2,000 and 3,000.[17] Regardless, the city was likely swollen with people answering the census, so it may have been a larger number than archaeological records suggest. For this reason, some archaeologists place the population as high as 10,000 people.

Interestingly, three different sources place the number of babies slaughtered at far larger numbers than the population of Bethlehem. The Greek liturgy says that 14,000 boys were killed. The Syrians claim 64,000 boys were slaughtered. Coptic sources state that there were 144,000 babies killed.[18] Regardless of the number of boys slaughtered, Herod regarded their lives as unimportant.

---

[16] William F. Albright and C.S. Mann, *Matthew: A New Translation with Introduction and Commentary* (New York: Doubleday, 1971), 19.
[17] https://scholar.lib.vt.edu/VA-news/VA-Pilot/issues/1994/vp941215/12150643.htm Accessed September 22, 2024.
[18] https://www.newadvent.org/cathen/07419a.htm Accessed September 21, 2024.

Herod's Insecure Foundations

The root of Herod's murderous tendencies was his misplaced security. If your security rests in anything or anyone other than God, you will not be secure. The world is unpredictable, the economy is unpredictable, politics are unpredictable, people are unpredictable; but our God is the same, yesterday, today, and forever.[19] This is what we can learn from Herod. Psalm 20:7 says, "Some trust in chariots and some in horses, but we trust in the name of the LORD our God." There is only one thing that we can be secure in, and that is the redeeming love of God. If we place our security in anything outside Him, we will never be satisfied. We will always be worried for our own good. Placing his hope in the temporal world led Herod into a life of sin and death. Placing our hope in the love of our LORD and Savior will lead to eternal life.

What would this look like today? What is your hope in? We all tend to place our trust in something other than God. Perhaps it's a job that you justify spending more hours at than you should. Perhaps it's your financial security. Perhaps you feverishly watch the stock market every day. Maybe you don't tithe because you worry you won't have enough money. Maybe your trust is in the government, to the point that you have lost relationships with those who don't vote the same as you. Herod murdered countless thousands during his fruitless quest for earthly security. It would be easy to hold ourselves above this despicable, evil man. But consider that the depths of his destruction were only because he had the power to ruthlessly murder his enemies. What have we destroyed within our own sphere of influence in a quest for earthly security? Perhaps you have massacred the peace of your family or sacrificed your marriage. Regardless of where you place your hope, we must trust in the name of the Lord our God.

Satan is the great deceiver. He loves to twist the truth. The first words out of his mouth back in Genesis were a lie. But like any good liar, the lie is based in truth but twisted ever so slightly. He loves to suggest lies to us to increase our anxiety and our fear. This reduces our reliance on God and

---

[19] Hebrews 13:8, "Jesus Christ is the same yesterday and today and forever."

steals our joy. Therefore, we must place all of our trust in God. This trust in an all-knowing, all-powerful Father brings a peace that surpasses understanding.[20] It is a peace that says, "no matter what comes, you are safe in the hands of the Father."

This does not mean that Christians will never experience tragedy or loss. It means that ultimately, our earthly needs and our eternity are secure in Christ. Even if we lose our very lives,[21] we will be with the Lord, and we can take comfort in that. Herod never knew such a day of comfort or peace. His murderous rages reflected his sad and unquiet mind – always seeking earthly security that can only be found in the eternal. Place your trust in God and you will live with the tranquility that evaded Herod the Great.

---

[20] Philippians 4:6-7, "Do not be anxious about anything, but in everything by prayer and supplication with thanksgiving let your requests be made known to God. [7] And the peace of God, which surpasses all understanding, will guard your hearts and your minds in Christ Jesus."

[21] Matthew 16:25, "For whoever would save his life will lose it, but whoever loses his life for my sake will find it."

REVIEW QUESTIONS

1. Herod's constant concern for his throne is really not much different than many kings. What makes Herod so much worse than them?

2. What are some similarities and differences between Herod and Pharaoh?

3. In contrast to the insecurity displayed by Herod, Joseph's absolute trust in God was displayed when he obeyed without a second thought. Have you ever been asked to do something where you had to step out in faith? How did you respond?

4. Herod's hope was wrongly placed in his position as king. In what areas of your life do you wrongly place hope? In what things can your security be found? How can you change that?

5. Herod responded to threats to his earthly security with murder. What ways do we destroy lives as we seek security in earthly things?

6. Consider the following Psalms and comment on how they reflect on how we are to live.

    Psalm 31:14-15

    Psalm 37:4-6

    Psalm 40:4

    Psalm 112:7

Salome with the Head of John the Baptist, Artemisia Gentileschi.
Painting: oil on canvas, 1610-1615. Budapest: Museum of Fine Arts.

10

Herod Antipas and Herodias

MARK 6:17-29

17 For it was Herod who had sent and seized John and bound him in prison for the sake of Herodias, his brother Philip's wife, because he had married her. 18 For John had been saying to Herod. "It is not lawful for you to have your brother's wife." 19 And Herodias had a grudge against him and wanted to put him to death. But she could not, 20 for Herod feared John, knowing that he was a righteous and holy man, and he kept him safe. When he heard him, he was greatly perplexed, and yet he heard him gladly.

21 But an opportunity came when Herod on his birthday gave a banquet for his nobles and military commanders and the leading men of Galilee. 22 For when Herodias's daughter came in and danced, she *pleased Herod and his guests. And the king said to the girl, "Ask me for whatever you wish, and I will give it to you." *23* And he vowed to her, "Whatever you ask me, I will give you, up to half of my kingdom." *24* And she went out and said to her mother, "For what should I ask?" And she said, "The head of John the Baptist." *25* And she came in immediately with haste to the king and asked, saying, "I want you to give me at once the head of John the Baptist on a platter." *26* And the king was exceedingly sorry, but because of his oaths and his guests he did not want to break his word to her. *27* And immediately the king sent an executioner with orders to bring John's head. He went and beheaded him in the prison *28* and brought his head on a platter and gave it to the girl, and the girl gave it to her mother. *29* When his disciples heard of it, they came and took his body and laid it in a tomb.*

HISTORICALLY, THE ROYAL FAMILY OF England has nothing on the Herodian dynasty regarding violence and dysfunctional familial relationships. The story of Herodias' daughter, Salome,[1] asking for the head of John the Baptist on a platter is perhaps one of the most graphic descriptions of evil in all Scripture. Salome's mother, Herodias, was the one who instigated it. However, her stepfather, desiring to appease her mother and safe face with his party guests, granted this gruesome request.

---

[1] Salome was the daughter of Herod Antipas's brother Phillip. This would make her Antipas' niece. When Antipas married Herodias, Salome became his stepdaughter. Therefore, Salome was Antipas's niece and stepdaughter.

Herod Antipas

Herod Antipas (to avoid confusion with Herod the Great, I will refer to Herod Antipas as Antipas) was a surviving son of Herod the Great. Antipas was not a king, even though he referred to himself as such. He was merely a "tetrarch," a ruler of one-quarter of his father's territory. Antipas ruled Galilee and Perea for 43 years. Like his father, he was a prolific builder, responsible for building projects at Sepphoris and Betharamphtha and for constructing his capital, Tiberius, on the western shore of the Sea of Galilee. As the tetrarch of Galilee, it was Antipas who met with Jesus before He was crucified.[2] Technically, Antipas could be included in the Despicable Dozen for his interactions with Jesus. However, the events surrounding the death of John the Baptist seem more despicable.

The house of Antipas was a strange mixture of cold cruelty and superstition.[3] Like his father, Antipas was a descendant of Esau, therefore, not a Jew. However, since he ruled over the Jews, his religious beliefs were influenced by Jewish priests and prophets. One such individual who influenced Antipas was John the Baptist. But, like his father, Antipas would do anything necessary to protect his position of power.

Herod Antipas' Marriage to Herodias

Antipas' first wife was Phasaelis of Nabataea. However, she left him and returned home when she found out that Antipas intended to divorce her in order to marry his sister-in-law Herodias, a woman with whom he had an adulterous relationship. Herodias was the wife of Antipas' half-brother, Philip. Herodias and Philip had a daughter named Salome. Divorcing Phasaelis to marry his brother's wife would have been seen as highly scandalous,[4] on the level of the actions of Henry VIII of England with his bevy of wives.

---

[2] Luke 23:6-7, "When Pilate heard this, he asked whether the man was a Galilean. [7] And when he learned that He belonged to Herod's jurisdiction, he sent Him over to Herod, who was himself in Jerusalem at that time.".

[3] R. Alan Cole, *Mark*, TNTC (Grand Rapids: Eerdmans, 1989), 172.

[4] Philip was still alive when Antipas married Herodias.

Antipas' marriage to Herodias was condemned in the Mosaic law.[5] The only possible method to legitimize their union was in Levirate law. Levirate marriage laws can be found in Deuteronomy 25:5-6.[6] In the ancient Near East, it was a serious issue if a man died without having an heir. Levirate marriage sought to alleviate this by mandating a widow marry her dead husband's brother. When this happened, the first son of the new marriage was considered to be the child of the dead man. This would preserve the family line of a man who died without offspring. It was essential in Israel at the time that a man should have male offspring to carry on the family name and inherit his property.[7]

There were two issues with Antipas and Herodias claiming Levirate marriage laws. Firstly, Herodias had a daughter, Salome. According to Josephus, Salome married her cousin Aristobulus of Chalcis, thus becoming queen of Armenia Minor.[8] Since Salome was an heir, it would fall upon her husband to support Herodias. Levirate law only applied if there was no heir.

The second issue with their marriage was that Antipas's half-brother, Philip, was still alive. Even if Philip was dead, it would have been illegal for Antipas to marry his brother's wife. The fact Philip was still alive made Antipas' marriage even more appalling. Therefore, his marriage to Herodias was adulterous, incestuous, and bigamous.[9]

The conflict between Herodias and John the Baptist began when John openly condemned the relationship between Herod Antipas and Herodias.

---

[5] Leviticus 18:16, "You shall not uncover the nakedness of your brother's wife; it is your brother's nakedness." Leviticus 20:21, "If a man takes his brother's wife, it is impurity. He has uncovered his brother's nakedness; they shall be childless."

[6] Deuteronomy 25:5-6, "If brothers dwell together, and one of them dies and has no son, the wife of the dead man shall not be married outside the family to a stranger. Her husband's brother shall go in to her and take her as his wife and perform the duty of a husband's brother to her. [6] And the first son whom she bears shall succeed to the name of his dead brother, that his name may not be blotted out of Israel."

[7] Timothy J. Mulder, *Ruth: A Story of God's Redeeming Love* (Corpus Christi: Armchair Theology, 2023), 66.

[8] Flavius Josephus, *The Complete Works* (Nashville: Thomas Nelson, 1998), 582.

[9] Cole, 173.

John confronted Antipas about his affair and his marriage to Herodias.[10] According to the gospel of Matthew, it was John the Baptist's bold condemnation of this arrangement that led Herod Antipas to have him arrested.[11] Many people likely condemned Antipas and Herodias behind closed doors. But John had no qualms about denouncing them in public. This spelled political trouble for the royal couple.

John's confrontation of Antipas and Herodias was not political. His desire was for them to come to repentance. Even though Herod Antipas did not adhere to Jewish religious practices, he was intrigued by John and his message. But Antipas' lust for Herodias would not allow him to correct his fault. If he repented, he would no longer have a relationship with Herodias. He valued that more than he did a right relationship with God. Herod Antipas chose the sins of the flesh over salvation. Having imprisoned John, the royal couple could continue their adulterous and incestuous relationship without unwanted publicity.

Herodias openly wanted John killed because he condemned her marriage to Antipas. She knew that "the only place where her marriage certificate could safely be written was on the back of the death warrant of John the Baptist."[12] Herodias was furious with John. During his imprisonment, she held a grudge against him and bode her time until the moment arrived when she could have John killed.

Antipas had John arrested "for the sake of Herodias."[13] However, Antipas did not kill John, for he knew that John was a man of God.[14]

---

[10] Mark 6:18, "For John had been saying to Herod, 'It is not lawful for you to have your brother's wife.'"

[11] Matthew 14:3, "For Herod had seized John and bound him and put him in prison for the sake of Herodias, his brother Philip's wife."

[12] T.W. Manson, *The Servant Messiah* (London: Cambridge University Press, 1953), 40.

[13] Matthew 14:3, "For Herod had seized John and bound him and put him in prison *for the sake of Herodias*, his brother Philip's wife." (Italics added.)

[14] Mark 6:20, "for Herod feared John, knowing that he was a righteous and holy man, and he kept him safe. When he heard him, he was greatly perplexed, and yet he heard him gladly."

Antipas walked the middle ground by trying to appease his wife and keep John safe.[15]

Salome's Dance

Antipas threw himself a birthday party and held a banquet to which he invited his nobles, military commanders, and the social elite from Galilee.[16] These were the people he needed to keep happy and impress to remain in power. However, the combination of a party atmosphere, plenty of alcohol, and the general debauchery in Antipas' court led to the death of John the Baptist.

Herodias' daughter, Salome, came and danced for her stepfather/uncle, Herod Antipas. Most accounts of her dance maintain it was an erotic dance.[17] While erotic dancing is a behavior unbecoming a princess (especially given that Salome was his niece and step-daughter) the low moral standards of Antipas' court would not be inconsistent with it.[18] Salome's performance pleased Antipas and his intoxicated guests. His impaired judgment led Antipas to make the horrible vow in verse 23[19]. Trying to impress his party guests, Antipas made a foolish and braggadocious vow offering Salome up to half of his kingdom.[20] Salome ran to her mother Herodias and inquired what she should ask for.[21] Herodias didn't even hesitate to respond – this despicable queen knew

---

[15] See previous footnote on Mark 6:20.

[16] Mark 6:21-22, "But an opportunity came when Herod on his birthday gave a banquet for his nobles and military commanders and the leading men of Galilee. [22] For when Herodias's daughter came in and danced, she pleased Herod and his guests."

[17] Walter W. Wessel, and Mark L. Strauss, *Matthew and Mark,* TEBC (Grand Rapids: Zondervan, 2010), 787.

[18] Wessel and Strauss, 787.

[19] Mark 6:23, "Whatever you ask me, I will give you, up to half of my kingdom."

[20] What is ironic is that Herod offered her up to "half of his kingdom," yet he was not a king. He served Rome. The kingdom belonged to Rome, not him.

[21] Mark 6:24, "And she went out and said to her mother, 'For what should I ask?' And she said, 'The head of John the Baptist.'"

exactly what she wanted.[22] She jumped at the opportunity to get revenge and silence John forever.

There is an uncanny resemblance between Antipas, Herodias, and John's relationship to that of Ahab, Jezebel, and Elijah. Both evil couples wanted the prophet who called them out for their sins to be executed. In both cases, the queen was the more evil of the two, with Jezebel displaying hate for Elijah because he stood up against the false god Baal. Herodias likewise hated John the Baptist because he stood up against her adulterous marriage to Antipas. Both kings were weak leaders who often caved to their wives' spiteful demands.

What about us? What happens when we say to anything, "Ask whatever you wish and I will give it to you?" Do we say that to a spouse? Do we say that to a supervisor at work? Do we say it to someone we are trying to impress? That promise smacks of idolatry. When we are willing to give everything we have to something, it has a disproportionately important place in our lives. "When we say to anyone except God, 'Ask whatever you wish and I will give it to you,' it costs too much."[23]

John's Head on a Platter

According to verse 25,[24] Salome, at Herodias' urging, requested the head of John the Baptist on a platter. Immediately, Antipas regretted[25] making the promise, but knew he had been trapped. He had a quandary: should he execute John, a prophet he believed to be just and holy, or lose face with his nobles and military leaders?

---

[22] Author Commentary: Herodias, by her request, displayed no concern for her daughter. It never occurred that her grotesque request was being made of a young girl. Parents today frequently worry about their children being exposed to violence in video games and movies. Herodias callously exposed her child to a bloody, severed head. She and Antipas should make the list of Despicable Parents as well.

[23] Buttrick, 735.

[24] Mark 6:25, "And she came in immediately with haste to the king and asked, saying, 'I want you to give me at once the head of John the Baptist on a platter.'"

[25] The Greek word in verse 26 is *perilypos*, meaning "greatly distressed" or "encompassingly sorrowful."

Antipas faced the question, "Is it better to break a foolish promise than to carry it out and sin?" He caved under the social pressure.[26] This is often the case with the gospel: its message may be unwelcome, but it pricks the conscience. Instead of acquiescing, Antipas could have apologized and refused her request. But Antipas was more conscious of those in his presence than he was with the Lord's presence. Antipas was more concerned about what others thought of him than what God thought of him. He was too proud to admit his mistake. Antipas did not hesitate to impress his guests.[27] Once again, violence served as the answer to a moral dilemma.

Regret vs. Repentance

We know that Antipas had a healthy fear of John the Baptist.[28] Regardless of his actions, he believed that John was a just and holy man, and, according to verse 20, Antipas was intrigued by John the Baptist. He had heard John preach,[29] but it was Herodias who pushed him to imprison and ultimately execute John.

Antipas was haunted by what he had done to John the Baptist. He felt so much regret that he succumbed to superstitious conspiracy theories that Jesus was John the Baptist raised from the dead.[30] However, all this regret was not enough to cause him to repent. Regret and repentance are two different things. Regret is feeling remorse for one's sins. Regret is a worldly sorrow. It says, "I'm sorry I got caught." Repentance is a sincere

---

[26] Mark 6:26, "And the king was exceedingly sorry, but because of his oaths and his guests he did not want to break his word to her."

[27] Mark 6:27-28, "And immediately the king sent an executioner with orders to bring John's head. He went and beheaded him in the prison [28] and brought his head on a platter and gave it to the girl, and the girl gave it to her mother."

[28] Herod's fear was not akin to dread but was a voluntary respect for John.

[29] According to Matthew Henry, this was a condescension on Herod's part, considering John's appearance.

[30] Matthew 14:1-2, "At that time Herod the tetrarch heard about the fame of Jesus, and he said to his servants, "This is John the Baptist. He has been raised from the dead; that is why these miraculous powers are at work in him."

turning away from sin and a turning toward God. It is a godly sorrow for one's transgressions. It says, "I'm sorry I sinned against you, O God."

The Westminster Confession of Faith 15.2 says, "In this repentance the sinner is able to see his sins as God sees them, as filthy and hateful, and as involving great danger to the sinner, because they are completely contrary to the holy nature and righteous law of God. Understanding that God in Christ is merciful to those who repent, the sinner suffers deep sorrow for and hates his sins, and so he determines to turn away from all of them. And turning to God, he tries to walk with Him according to all His commandments."

It is not uncommon for people under the influence of alcohol or drugs to cave to peer pressure and make grievous mistakes. While beheading someone on a whim at a drunken party may be outside our normal experience, it is not uncommon for people to commit other sins in such circumstances. Are we really so different when alcohol and partying lead to domestic violence, infidelity or other consequences that descend with crushing regret the next day? Indeed, driving under the influence may seem like a victimless crime until someone innocent is killed in a car accident. The slippery slope of sin accelerates and our consciences are suppressed when we decide to use substances or hang out with people who are of questionable character. In that way, we are exactly like Antipas.

Perhaps you are thinking that none of this applies to you. Are you blessed to have never struggled with alcohol or drugs? But caving to peer pressure does not always involve substance abuse. If we care more about what people think than what God thinks, then peer pressure will lead us to sin anywhere – online, school, the workplace, at church or even in our own homes. It takes strength of character to stand firm under the onslaught of peer pressure. We can only do so when fortified by the Holy Spirit and buoyed by the Word. But it helps to surround ourselves with friends of good influence and to avoid situations or people where such temptations are likely to occur. We must be more concerned with what God thinks of us than what man thinks. Paul tells us, in Galatians 1:10, "For am I now seeking the approval of man, or of God? Or am I trying to please man? If

I were still trying to please man, I would not be a servant of Christ." As children of God, we are called to fear God, not men. What God thinks of us is far more important than what others think of us or what we think of ourselves.

REVIEW QUESTIONS

1. How did Herodias' actions display her disregard for her daughter's well-being?

2. What is the difference between regret and repentance?

3. Do you find yourself more concerned about what others think than what God thinks? In which areas of your life are you most susceptible to peer pressure? How can you change this?

4. Have you ever sinned because of peer pressure or to save face? What were the consequences?

5. What are some other Biblical examples of rash vows? What were the consequences?

6. Do you ever consider how your sins affect your children?

7. Consider the following verses and comment on how they reflect on how we are to live.

    Proverbs 13:20

    Romans 10:12

    2 Timothy 3:1-5

Pilate Washing His Hands, Hendrick Ter Brugghen. Painting: oil on canvas, 1615-1628. Gateshead: Shipley Art Gallery.

11

Pontius Pilate

MATTHEW 27:11-26

11 Now Jesus stood before the governor, and the governor asked Him, "Are you the King of the Jews?" Jesus said, "You have said so." 12 But when He was accused by the chief priests and elders, He gave no answer. 13 Then Pilate said to Him, "Do you not hear how many things they testify against you?" 14 But He gave him no answer, not even to a single charge, so that the governor was greatly amazed.

15 Now at the feast, the governor was accustomed to release for the crowd any one prisoner whom they wanted. 16 And they had then a notorious prisoner called Barabbas. 17 So when they had gathered, Pilate said to them, *"Whom do you want me to release for you: Barabbas, or Jesus who is called Christ?"* [18] *For he knew that it was out of envy that they had delivered Him up.* [19] *Besides, while he was sitting on the judgment seat, his wife sent word to him, "Have nothing to do with that righteous man, for I have suffered much because of Him today in a dream."* [20] *Now the chief priests and the elders persuaded the crowd to ask for Barabbas and destroy Jesus.* [21] *The governor again said to them, "Which of the two do you want me to release for you?" And they said, "Barabbas."* [22] *Pilate said to them, "Then what shall I do with Jesus who is called Christ?" They all said, "Let Him be crucified!"* [23] *And he said, "Why? What evil has He done?" But they shouted all the more, "Let Him be crucified!"*

[24] *So when Pilate saw that he was gaining nothing, but rather that a riot was beginning, he took water and washed his hands before the crowd, saying, "I am innocent of this man's blood; see to it yourselves."* [25] *And all the people answered, "His blood be on us and on our children!"* [26] *Then he released for them Barabbas, and having scourged Jesus, delivered Him to be crucified.*

THE PRIMARY ISSUE IN THE above Scripture is in determining who is more despicable. We have three choices:

1. Pilate, who refused to adequately administer justice to Jesus, opting instead to appease a mob, even if it meant killing an innocent man.
2. The chief priests and the elders, who plotted against Jesus, paid false witnesses, and conducted an illegal, sham trial. Here, they incited the people to cry out for the crucifixion of Jesus.

3. The crowd who, just five days before, chanted, "Hosanna to the Son of David! Blessed is He who comes in the name of the Lord! Hosanna in the highest!"[1] Now, they demanded that Jesus be crucified.

The actions of all three parties, Pilate, the chief priests and elders, and the crowd were all despicable. The influence of politics and a riotous mob aside, Pilot was legally responsible, even if he tried to wash his hands of it.

Pontius Pilate

According to Matthew 27:2,[2] Pilate was the governor (or prefect[3]) over Judea and Samaria. Pilate was appointed prefect by Tiberius Caesar in 26 AD. The governor usually lived in Caesarea but would move to Jerusalem during festivals. Pilate had come from Caesarea to maintain order during Passover.

Politically, Pilate was like most politicians – worried about self-preservation. He was less concerned about justice than keeping the argumentative Jews peaceful. Pilot exhibited a typical Roman disdain for Jewish laws and customs.[4] As such, his hatred of the Jews caused him to be a cruel and aggressive ruler. For example, he stole money from the temple to pay for aqueducts. When the Jews protested, he sent Roman soldiers to massacre them. Eventually, the Jews complained about Pilate directly to Caesar, and in 36 AD, he was recalled to Rome.

---

[1] Matthew 21:9, "And the crowds that went before Him and that followed Him were shouting, "Hosanna to the Son of David! Blessed is He who comes in the name of the Lord! Hosanna in the highest!"

[2] Matthew 27:2, "So they bound Him, led Him away and handed Him over to Pilate the governor."

[3] A prefect was a civil or military official in ancient Rome. Prefects typically oversaw small, troubled areas of the Roman empire. Another obligation of the prefect was the sole authority to condemn and sentence criminals.

[4] Alfred Plummer, *An Exegetical Commentary on the Gospel According to Matthew* (Grand Rapids: Eerdmans, 1956), 390.

Judea was a bit of a thorn in Rome's side. Rome ruled by "Romanizing" their provinces, offering citizenship and bringing the Roman lifestyle, including building programs, providing roads, clean water, sanitation, bath houses, and amphitheaters offering gladiatorial games. Roman policy was tolerant of local customs and religions. A polytheistic society, Rome frequently ended up incorporating local gods into the pantheon[5] that they worshiped. Additionally, bringing Roman government and commerce was almost always advantageous to conquered territories. This made Roman imperial expansion hugely successful, and in general, avoided the need for prolonged military occupation. In the case of the Jews, this had backfired spectacularly. The isolationist and staunchly monotheistic practices of the Jews were downright baffling to the Roman mindset. Their refusal to come quietly into the Roman fold made Judea a hotbed of violent rebellion. Judea was not a posh assignment for friends of Caesar or the Senate. It was a difficult military posting in a desert backwater. To have any hope of furthering his career, Pilate needed to rule it with an iron first.

Are You The King of the Jews?

Early in the morning, before Jesus was brought to Pilate, the chief priests and elders (Sanhedrin[6]) asked the Romans to sentence Jesus to death. They were required to bring Jesus to Pilate because only the Romans could carry out the death penalty. Jesus' trial occurred on a raised platform outside Pilate's residence so the public could view it. John Calvin said: "The Son of God *stood,* as a criminal, before a mortal man, and there permitted Himself to be accused and condemned, that we may *stand* boldly before God."[7] (Italics added.)

---

[5] Pantheon refers to two things: a group of gods and goddesses; or, the temple in Rome where they were worshiped. In this case, it refers to the former.

[6] The Sanhedrin was the Jewish supreme court, comprising 23 or 71 rabbis. They settled both religious and civil matters.

[7] John Calvin, *Calvin's Commentaries*, XVII (Grand Rapids: Baker, 1993), 275.

When the Sanhedrin presented Jesus to Pilate, they used the title "King of the Jews" to bias Pilate against Jesus for political reasons. They were trying to deceive Pilate into thinking that Jesus was a revolutionary who sought to overthrow Roman rule. Jesus was indeed King of the Jews, but not in the way Pilate understood.[8] Pilate's goal was to determine if Jesus was a risk to foment rebellion. If Pilate found *any* evidence that Jesus disturbed the peace, he would have condemned Him without delay. However, he found none. Upon looking at Jesus, Pilate knew He was no threat to Rome. Pilate's concern was whether or not Jesus had broken Roman law and he knew that Jesus had not done so. Pilate saw through the Sanhedrin's plans. He knew that this was a religious matter and, as such, was not his responsibility. Pilate remained unimpressed with the weak case against Jesus, and he was well aware of Jesus' popularity among the people and the jealousy that this instilled in the chief priests and elders.[9] Additionally, he knew that the Jews would not turn someone over to the Roman authorities if they thought he could lead a successful revolution and overturn Roman rule.[10]

Crucifixion was a serious punishment that the Romans did not hesitate to employ. As execution and torture, it was designed to send a message to the people under Roman rule. But that does not mean it would be without consequence to apply it to a case of non-violent religious disagreement.

If Jesus had remained silent, He would have been condemned by Roman law since the defense rested heavily upon the defendant's testimony. Roman authorities disliked sentencing an undefended man.

---

[8] John goes into greater detail about this in his Gospel: John 18:34-37, "Jesus answered, 'Do you say this of your own accord, or did others say it to you about me?' [35] Pilate answered, 'Am I a Jew? Your own nation and the chief priests have delivered you over to me. What have you done?' [36] Jesus answered, 'My kingdom is not of this world. If my kingdom were of this world, my servants would have been fighting, that I might not be delivered over to the Jews. But my kingdom is not from the world.' [37] Then Pilate said to Him, 'So you are a king?' Jesus answered, 'You say that I am a king. For this purpose, I was born and for this purpose I have come into the world—to bear witness to the truth. Everyone who is of the truth listens to my voice.'"

[9] Craig L. Blomberg, *Matthew* TNAC (Nashville: Broadman, 1992), 410.

[10] D.A. Carson, *God With Us: Themes from Matthew* (Eugene: Wipf and Stock, 1995), 160.

Defendants were offered three opportunities to respond to their charges before being convicted of their crimes. Pilate clearly believed Jesus to be innocent and urged him to defend himself and was surprised when Jesus didn't.

Charles Spurgeon said, "Pilate was really anxious to deliver Christ from his cruel enemies; but like most wicked men, he was a great coward, so he attempted to gain his end by a crafty artifice."[11] According to Luke 23:4-6,[12] Pilate sent Jesus to Herod Antipas to be judged. Pilate wanted to know if Herod saw Jesus as a threat to Roman authority. Pilot may have hoped Herod would convict Jesus and thus absolve him of further responsibility. But Herod Antipas treated Jesus with contempt and mocked Him.[13] Herod refused to pass judgment on Jesus. So before long, Jesus was back and Pilate was running out of options.

Caving in to the Crowd
When Jesus returned from Herod, Pilate took a different approach. He was still trying to get out of condemning an innocent man. Pilate turned to the Jewish tradition of releasing one criminal during Passover. This was a foolish and improper practice and was an abuse of the Passover celebration. Nothing could be more unreasonable than celebrating Passover by allowing crimes to go unpunished.[14]

---

[11]Charles H. Spurgeon, *The Gospel of the Kingdom: A Commentary on the Book of Matthew* (Pasadena: Pilgrim,1996), 245.

[12] Luke 23:4-7, "Then Pilate announced to the chief priests and the crowd, 'I find no basis for a charge against this man.' [5] But they insisted, 'He stirs up the people all over Judea by His teaching. He started in Galilee and has come all the way here.' [6] On hearing this, Pilate asked if the man was a Galilean. [7] When he learned that Jesus was under Herod's jurisdiction, he sent Him to Herod, who was also in Jerusalem at that time."

[13] Luke 23:8-12, "When Herod saw Jesus, he was very glad, for he had long desired to see Him, because he had heard about Him, and he was hoping to see some sign done by Him. [9] So he questioned Him at some length, but He made no answer. [10] The chief priests and the scribes stood by, vehemently accusing Him. [11] And Herod with his soldiers treated Him with contempt and mocked Him. Then, arraying Him in splendid clothing, he sent Him back to Pilate. [12] And Herod and Pilate became friends with each other that very day, for before this they had been at enmity with each other."

[14] Calvin, 282.

So, Pilate selected a notorious prisoner, Barabbas, to set free. Barabbas, whose name means "son of the father" in Hebrew, was described by Mark as a rebel involved in a recent insurrection.[15] Pilate gave the crowd their choice of whom to release, Jesus or Barabbas. The crowd, inflamed by the chief priests and elders, chose Barabbas. All four Gospels agree that the Jews preferred a convicted murderer over Jesus. By choosing Barabbas over Jesus, Christ was placed lower than an insurrectionist and a murderer.[16] According to Mark 15:9-12,[17] Pilate, to push the crowd a little more, claimed that even the crowd called him King of the Jews. The crowd replied to Pilate, "We have no king but Caesar!"[18] In verse 19, Pilate's wife, Procla, sent word to him warning him about a dream she had about Jesus. Pilate, however, was too insecure to listen to his wife's intuition,[19] instead bowing to the crowd's demands.

Pilate then asked what the crowd wanted him to do with Jesus. Until now, Pilate had tried to protect Jesus' innocence. Frustrated and no longer acting rationally, he caved to the mob's demands. The crowd responded, "Crucify Him!" Pilate then proposed a compromise to have Him scourged and released.[20] Scourging involved using a *flagellum*, a multi-tailed whip with pieces of bone, iron, or spikes attached to the ends. The flagellum was designed to rip into the naked flesh of the victim's back. Scourging frequently ended in death. Jesus was scourged before Pilate rendered a

---

[15] Mark 15:7, "And among the rebels in prison, who had committed murder in the insurrection, there was a man called Barabbas."

[16] Even though Christ was the opposite of a murderer. He brought people back to life.

[17] Mark 15:9-12, "And he answered them, saying, 'Do you want me to release for you the King of the Jews?' [10] For he perceived that it was out of envy that the chief priests had delivered Him up. [11] But the chief priests stirred up the crowd to have him release for them Barabbas instead. [12] And Pilate again said to them, 'Then what shall I do with the man you call the King of the Jews?'"

[18] John 19:15, "They cried out, 'Away with Him, away with Him, crucify Him!' Pilate said to them, 'Shall I crucify your King?' The chief priests answered, 'We have no king but Caesar.'"

[19] That would have made for awkward dinner conversation. In my experience, ignoring your wife's words of caution can lead to an "I told you so!" of migraine proportions.

[20] Luke 23:16, "I will therefore punish and release Him."

verdict.[21] Pilate hoped that this punishment would satisfy the crowd and that Jesus would not have to be killed. Next, Pilate tried to remand Him to the Jewish authorities.[22] He remonstrated before pronouncing Jesus' sentence.[23] In summary, the Roman government, as far as Pilate was concerned, had not consented to the execution of Jesus.

The Verdict

Up to this point, Pilate had conducted Jesus' trial fairly and in accordance with Roman law. It wasn't illegal to flog Jesus because He wasn't a Roman citizen. In fact, beliefs in the ancient Near East were that it was impossible to get a confession without torture. But Pilate had exhausted his options to find Jesus innocent and was likely at the end of his patience in dealing with the tempestuous crowd. He announced Christ's innocence but agreed to punish Him *as if* He had been found guilty. The chief priests and the elders had convicted Jesus of blasphemy, but they could not execute the death sentence without Pilate's help. Unable to restrain the riotous crowd, Pilate yielded to their furious demands. The mob mentality overran Pilate's authority.

Pilate was not motivated by justice but by fear of an agitated mob. Pilate feared a riot more than he feared the injustice of condemning an innocent man. He could have released Jesus, but his future with Rome depended on whether or not he could maintain the peace. He decided that his political future was more important than the demands of justice.[24]

In verse 24, Pilate washed his hands of the decision. This was not a Roman practice. As much as he despised the Jews, Pilate was clearly

---

[21] Luke 23:22, "A third time he said to them, 'Why? What evil has He done? I have found in Him no guilt deserving death. I will therefore punish and release Him.' (I know the verse in this footnote is almost identical to the previous one. However, this emphasizes that Pilate believed that Jesus was innocent and that he was punishing Him to appease the crowd.)

[22] John 18:31, "Pilate said to them, 'Take Him yourselves and judge Him by your own law.' The Jews said to him, 'It is not lawful for us to put anyone to death.'"

[23] John 18:38b, "After he had said this, he went back outside to the Jews and told them, 'I find no guilt in Him.'"

[24] Carson, 160.

exposed to the Scriptures and Jewish beliefs and customs. Handwashing was a ritual prescribed in Deuteronomy 21:6-9.[25] In these verses, the leaders of Israel washed their hands to declare their innocence of the blood of a slain man. This was, in Jewish tradition, how you would demonstrate your innocence. Pilate's actions were understood to say that he disagreed with the verdict. It was meant to taunt the Jews. And then, the angry mob shouted, "His blood be on us and on our children." Pilate had taken a Jewish ceremony and contemptuously used it against them. Calvin asks, "How could a few drops of water wash away the stain of a crime which no satisfaction of any kind could obliterate?"[26] Spurgeon says, "Pilate, you need something stronger than *water* to wash *the blood* of that *just person* off your hands." (Italics added.)[27]

Pilate, like Herod the Great, was more worried about his precarious position of power. He looked out for himself. Even if it meant ordering the death of an innocent man. Pilate, like Herod Antipas, was more worried about what others thought of him than what God thought. In caving to the crowd's demands, Pilate violated his conscience. He knew what was right and what was wrong, but in the end, he did the wrong thing. He had corrupted his office, which until now had been seen as relatively fair, as he walked the fine line between the Jews and Rome. Pilate tried to pass the buck by having Herod convict Jesus. He ignored the caution of his wife. Pilate deliberately did the wrong thing because he was more concerned about the crowd and ultimately his position in the Roman political structure.

---

[25] Deuteronomy 21:6-9, "And all the elders of that city nearest to the slain man shall wash their hands over the heifer whose neck was broken in the valley, [7] and they shall testify, 'Our hands did not shed this blood, nor did our eyes see it shed. [8] Accept atonement, O LORD, for your people Israel, whom you have redeemed, and do not set the guilt of innocent blood in the midst of your people Israel, so that their blood guilt be atoned for.' [9] So you shall purge the guilt of innocent blood from your midst, when you do what is right in the sight of the LORD."
[26] Calvin, 287.
[27] Charles Spurgeon, *Commentary on Matthew* (Edinburgh: Banner of Truth Trust, 2010), 246.

How often do we, like Pilate, when faced with a decision between right and wrong, let the pressure of others push us to make the wrong decision? How do we know which decision is the correct decision? Outside influences on our values can be powerful. We must remember that when we are tempted to intentionally make a wrong choice, as Pilate did, that God will provide a way out.[28]

In deciding which decision is correct, we should pause from what we are doing, step back, and look at the situation from God's perspective. How do we know what God's perspective is? There are three things that we can do to determine what He would have us do: pray, spend time in God's Word, and seek godly counsel. Prayer is critical, as we enter into a quiet time of reflection and conversation with our God. 1 Peter 3:12 tells us, "For the eyes of the Lord are on the righteous, and His ears are open to their prayer. But the face of the Lord is against those who do evil." God hears our prayers and turns His face from evil.

Spending time in God's Word is another way to determine a godly perspective. I once had a friend tell me, "I've prayed, but I haven't heard from God." I asked when they last read their Bible. They responded, "I don't know." We cannot expect to hear from God if our Bibles are closed. Open up your Bible and see what God has to say to you.

Seeking the counsel of older Christians is also an excellent way to determine what God would have you do. Older Christians will have a seasoned perspective that may be grounded in experience. Chances are that they have faced some of the same dilemmas you have. Don't be afraid to ask them; they would be honored to help you.

Unlike Pilate, who ignored the council of others, and decided based on the emotions of himself and the unruly crowd, we are to seek God's face when confronted with major decisions. God will give us direction if we ask Him. His Word assures us of that.

---

[28] 1 Corinthians 10:13, "No temptation has overtaken you that is not common to man. God is faithful, and He will not let you be tempted beyond your ability, but with the temptation He will also provide the way of escape, that you may be able to endure it."

REVIEW QUESTIONS

1. What do you make of Pilate's wife's dream? How could Pilate have responded to her concerns? Is there someone in your life whom you have learned to trust their intuition?

2. What are the three ways that the author suggested to ascertain God's will when we are faced with difficult decisions?

3. What are other examples from Scripture where someone compromised their integrity? What were the consequences? How did God use their actions to further His will?

4. Have you ever compromised your integrity or been tempted to? What could you have done differently?

5. When overcoming addiction, people are often counseled to consider times when they know they will be tempted and prepare their response in advance. How does 1 Corinthians 10:13 underscore the need to prepare for temptation? What are some ways that we can prepare a way out?

6. What do the following verses say about seeking God's direction?

    2 Chronicles 7:14

    Psalm 119:105

    James 1:5-6

Last Supper, Carl Bloch. Painting: oil on copper plate, 1876.
Hillerød: Fredricksborg Castle. (Note: a portion of the painting has been
cropped by the author to avoid a Second Commandment violation.)

12

Judas Iscariot

JOHN 12:1-8

Six days before the Passover, Jesus therefore came to Bethany, where Lazarus was, whom Jesus had raised from the dead. ² So they gave a dinner for Him there. Martha served, and Lazarus was one of those reclining with Him at table. ³ Mary therefore took a pound of expensive ointment made from pure nard and anointed the feet of Jesus and wiped His feet with her hair. The house was filled with the fragrance of the perfume. ⁴ But Judas Iscariot, one of His disciples (he who was about to betray Him), said, ⁵ "Why was this ointment not sold for three hundred denarii and given to the poor?" ⁶ He said this, not because he cared about the poor, but because he was a thief, and having charge of the moneybag he used to help himself to what was put into it. ⁷ Jesus said, "Leave her alone, so that she may keep it for the day of my burial. [8] For the poor you always have with you, but you do not always have me."

MATTHEW 26:48-50

Now the betrayer had given them a sign, saying, "The one I will kiss is the man; seize Him." [49] And he came up to Jesus at once and said, "Greetings, Rabbi!" And he kissed Him. [50] Jesus said to him, "Friend do what you came to do." Then they came up and laid hands upon Jesus and seized Him.

MATTHEW 27:3-5

Then when Judas, His betrayer, saw that Jesus was condemned, he changed his mind and brought back the thirty pieces of silver to the chief priests and the elders, [4] saying, "I have sinned by betraying innocent blood." They said, "What is that to us? See to it yourself." [5] And throwing down the pieces of silver into the temple, he departed, and he went and hanged himself.

UPON LEARNING OF THE CONTENT of this book, *The Despicable Dozen*, you probably immediately thought of Judas Iscariot. He is indeed the poster-child of betrayal. But the Bible includes villains, not just to be antagonists, but also for what we can learn from them. Judas will forever go down in infamy for betraying Jesus Christ, a man with whom he followed like a brother for three years. He witnessed countless miracles, healings, and exorcisms. He heard many sermons, Scripture readings, and debates with the religious leaders. He had the privilege of speaking face-to-face with the Son of God for three years, and yet, he was not loyal. Judas is the most notorious traitor in the Bible and, arguably, in all of history

The name Iscariot has three possible meanings. It may be derived from the Aramaic root word "liar." Another meaning refers to the city where he was from, Kerioth, which was in Southern Israel.[1] His name may also have been based on the Latin word *sicarius*, which means "dagger man," indicating that Judas may have been a zealot.[2]

The early church detested and scorned Judas.[3] In every New Testament list of the disciples, his name appears last. In Acts 1, his name is left off entirely, and when his name is listed, he is always tagged with his role as a betrayer or traitor. Judas was the opposite of a disciple – his loyalties lay not with Christ, but with Satan.

Not A Surprise

The events on the evening of the Last Supper and Jesus' betrayal did not surprise Jesus. John 13:1 makes it abundantly clear, "When Jesus knew that his hour had come to depart out of this world…" Jesus knew what was going to happen. His disciples, however, had no idea what lay in store for them. Except for Judas Iscariot, who had the idea of betraying Jesus placed

---

[1] This would make Judas the only disciple not from Galilee, and that may have contributed to him feeling like an outsider.

[2] Zealots were fanatical Jewish nationalists responsible for many uprisings against Rome. They believed that any measures used were justified in achieving their goal. Believing that the ends justify the means makes someone willing to break the law, even if innocents are hurt. One example of a zealot was Barabbas, the insurrectionist released in place of Jesus. Luke 23:25, "He released the man who had been thrown into prison for insurrection and murder, for whom they asked, but he delivered Jesus over to their will." Additionally, there was a group within the zealots called the Sicarii (Assassins). The Sicarii carried knives everywhere they went and killed anyone sympathetic to Rome. While Judas was likely not Sicarii, he may have been associated with those who were.

[3] John MacArthur, *John 12-21*, TMNTC (Chicago: Moody, 2008), 73.

in his heart by Satan. In Genesis 3:15,[4] God foretold that the offspring of Eve, Jesus, would triumph over the offspring of the serpent.

Before Judas was even born, his betrayal of Christ was a part of God's divine plan. Psalm 41:9[5] foretold Judas' actions. In this verse, David states that the traitor has lifted his heel against him. The verse likens a traitor to a treacherous horse lifting its heel to kick its master violently. John 12:6[6] tells us Judas was a thief.

When Jesus gathered with His disciples in the upper room, He knew that Judas would yield his spirit to Satan and betray Him. Jesus knew His time had come and knew what it entailed. He knew what lay ahead, and He went through with it anyway. The fact that He knew what was going to happen ahead of time makes His sacrifice all the more meaningful.

Washing Feet

In the first eight verses of John 12, Mary washed Jesus' feet with expensive oil and dried them with her hair. Roads in the time of Jesus were dusty and littered with manure, so it was common to wash a guest's feet before a meal. Since no one had washed Jesus' feet, Mary took it upon herself to do so. Mary's actions came from a loving heart. This was truly a service of love, which likely touched every soul in the room, save one.

In John 12:5, Judas was disgusted about the wasting of resources when Mary washed Jesus' feet with perfume, saying, "Why was this ointment not sold for three hundred denarii and given to the poor?" Judas' self-aggrandizing statement was not motivated by altruism but by greed. Interestingly, Judas, in his statement, had already calculated the price of the ointment. In Judas' eyes, the washing of Jesus' feet was a waste, while "giving it to the poor" would have been a much more responsible thing to

---

[4] Genesis 3:15, "I will put enmity between you and the woman, and between your offspring and her offspring; He shall bruise your head, and you shall bruise His heel."

[5] Psalm 41:9, "Even my close friend in whom I trusted, who ate my bread, has lifted his heel against me."

[6] John 12:6, "He said this, not because he cared about the poor, but because he was a thief, and having charge of the moneybag he used to help himself to what was put into it."

do. Mary didn't even use all of the oil. In verse 7,[7] Jesus instructed her to keep the rest of the oil to anoint His body for burial.

In his opening statement to the group, Judas was telling Mary how to take care of her finances. Who does that? Who goes to someone else's house and questions how they spend their money? His statement was embarrassingly rude. If that wasn't bad enough, he also questioned her faith. One of the responsibilities of believers is to take care of the poor. Judas displayed a fake piety with his statement, and Jesus called him out for it by saying, "leave her alone, so that she may keep it for the day of my burial. For the poor you always have with you, but you do not always have me."[8]

Judas wasn't concerned about Jesus or His dirty feet. In his mind, Mary's act, even though it displayed devotion to her Savior, was wasteful. And just as her actions revealed the content of her heart, Judas' reaction did the same. Judas was cold and unfeeling inside. While everyone else in the room was touched by Mary's actions, Judas' hard heart grew even more hard. So hard that he went to the chief priests and struck a deal.

The Kiss

Judas' betrayal of Christ was only the tip of the iceberg. Judas had been planning on betraying his Lord long before the actual event took place. Matthew 5:14-16[9] tells us that he planned it out with the chief priests and the elders. They hated Jesus and His disciples. They sought an opportunity to kill Jesus and that opportunity presented itself in the person of Judas Iscariot. Judas told the chief priests and elders that the one that he kissed would be the Christ.

---

[7] John 12:7, "Jesus said, 'Leave her alone, so that she may keep it for the day of my burial. For the poor you always have with you, but you do not always have me.'"
[8] John 12:7-8.
[9] Matthew 5:14-16, "Then one of the twelve, whose name was Judas Iscariot, went to the chief priests [15] and said, 'What will you give me if I deliver Him over to you?' And they paid him thirty pieces of silver. [16] And from that moment he sought an opportunity to betray Him."

Oftentimes, a kiss on the cheek was a way of greeting someone. It was a sign of respect, friendship, and honor. For a disciple who had followed his Rabbi for three years, a kiss was a common expression of devotion. Judas used a sign of love to betray his Master.

Though written 800 years before, King David clearly understood Jesus' pain at this betrayal. In Psalm 55:12-14, David wrote, "For it is not an enemy who taunts me— then I could bear it; it is not an adversary who deals insolently with me then I could hide from him. But it is you, a man, my equal, my companion, my familiar friend. We used to take sweet counsel together; within God's house we walked in the throng." Judas, by giving the Son of God a kiss, went down in infamy as a fraud and despicable traitor.

The Progression of Evil

John Calvin has said, "The lust of men is kindled into a fiercer flame by Satan's fan."[10] This was undoubtedly true for Judas Iscariot. Satan was the one who fanned the flame of evil in Judas' heart. Though Judas accompanied Jesus, he never gave his heart to Him. His heart, harder than iron, should have been softened by Christ's kindness.[11] Satan entered Judas, but he already held the throne of Judas' heart. Although Satan inspired Judas' betrayal, Judas was still responsible for his actions.

Judas' lack of loyalty to Christ had gone undetected by the other disciples. The disciples trusted Judas so much that they made him their treasurer. Judas hid his duplicity so well that not one of them suspected him. Jesus, in John 13:18,[12] stated that He knew whom He had chosen, indicating His foreknowledge that Judas would betray Him.

At the Last Supper, when Jesus offered the morsel to Judas, it was a mark of the divine love in which Jesus sought to overcome evil with good.

---

[10] John. Calvin, *John 12-21* Calvin's Commentaries (Grand Rapids: Baker, 1993), 55.
[11] Calvin, 71.
[12] John 13:18, "I am not speaking of all of you; I know whom I have chosen. But the Scripture will be fulfilled, 'He who ate my bread has lifted his heel against me.'"

In Jewish culture, eating bread at the table of a superior brought with it a pledge of loyalty. It was also a sign of trust and friendship. Jesus showed Judas kindness right up to the end. Judas, however, was immune to Christ's display of love. Instead of receiving the morsel in love, Judas' heart was hardened, and Satan possessed him. "One who is wholly evil cannot remain in the company of those who belong to Christ."[13] After sharing the morsel with Christ, Judas left the upper room to execute his despicable deed.

There is nothing that man or Satan can do to thwart God's sovereign will. Satan can try his best, but it will be of no avail. Calvin says, "But as He governs those whom He has chosen, all the engines which Satan can employ will not prevent them from persevering to the end with unshaken firmness."[14] "Even the treachery of Judas can only serve the redemptive purposes of the mission on which Jesus has been sent."[15]

Regret and Suicide

Judas was given every opportunity to repent. When Jesus washed the disciples' feet, He said, "One of you will betray me."[16] When the disciples pressed Jesus to know whom He meant, He looked Judas in the eye and said, "What you do, do quickly."[17] In doing so, He was saying that He knew of Judas' evil plans. He gave Judas one last chance to turn back. Sadly, Judas never responded to that final call for repentance.

---

[13] R.V.G. Tasker, *John: An Introduction and Commentary* TBC (Grand Rapids: Eerdmans, 1989), 159.

[14] Calvin, 63.

[15] Carson, 471. See also Romans 8:28, "And we know that for those who love God *all things* work together for good, for those who are called according to his purpose." (Italics added.)

[16] John 13:21, "After saying these things, Jesus was troubled in His spirit, and testified, "Truly, truly, I say to you, one of you will betray me."

[17] John 13:27, "Then after he had taken the morsel, Satan entered into him. Jesus said to him, "What you are going to do, do quickly."

Like the other disciples, Judas did not understand what Jesus meant when He said, "Destroy this temple, and in three days I will raise it up."[18] They didn't understand that Jesus was talking about Himself and predicting His own resurrection. Following Jesus' betrayal, Judas simply believed that his Rabbi was going to die and the guilt for it was all on him. He approached the chief priests and confessed to them. He tried to return the 30 pieces of silver, as if that could stop the events already in motion. Such a grievous sin with no apparent opportunity to repent left Judas with only one option: suicide. One of the commonalities among those who attempt or commit suicide is hopelessness. Judas was indeed hopeless. Had Judas known that Jesus would be alive again in three days, he might have waited and approached His Lord and begged forgiveness. But he didn't. Judas showed *remorse* for his actions when he attempted to return the blood money and then committed suicide, but *he did not repent*. Judas did not have the love of Christ in his heart. He tried to make it right, but he never sought the mercy of Christ.

Conclusion

In seminary, I was blessed to study under some of my theological heroes including Ligon Duncan, Derek Thomas, Guy Waters, and Sinclair Ferguson. Needless to say, I received a world-class education. But, as great as my education was, it was nothing compared to that of Judas. Judas spent three years face-to-face with God Himself. There can be no greater education than that. Except that Judas clearly did not take to heart the things he had been taught. James 1:23-24[19] likens Judas' failure in this area to a man who looks in the mirror and immediately forgets what he looks like.

---

[18] John 2:19.

[19] James 1:23-24, "For if anyone is a hearer of the word and not a doer, he is like a man who looks intently at his natural face in a mirror. 24 For he looks at himself and goes away and at once forgets what he was like."

Judas spent three years with a man who loved His creation so much that He willingly sacrificed Himself to save His chosen people. Today, there are people who attend church every Sunday, and yet remain unsaved. People can spend their entire lives in the church and still have hardened hearts. They appear to be pious, but on the inside, they are dead. How many in the church want to look like they have it all together? We may play the part of a devout Christian, but internally, we are far from Him. Judas, on the outside, appeared as devoted to Jesus as the other disciples. But inside, Satan had a firm grip on his heart. Simply spending time in church does not make you a Christian. You must repent and be born of the Spirit.[20] Have you neglected your opportunities to repent? Are you drowning in the sorrows of sin but have yet to come to the foot of the cross to seek the forgiveness Jesus freely offers? Come to Him today and repent. He will forgive you and welcome you into His family.

---

[20] John 3:6, "That which is born of the flesh is flesh, and that which is born of the Spirit is spirit."

REVIEW QUESTIONS

1. Was Judas to blame for his actions? Or was Satan to blame? Why do you think so?

2. Do you think that Judas' treachery was visible before the last supper? Were there clues as to the loyalties of his heart?

3. Did Judas harden his own heart? Or did God harden it? (Hint: How has this study strengthened your understanding of how God directs His sovereign will but is still not the author of evil?)

4. How are you like Judas, appearing devout on the outside, but fully corrupted by sin on the inside? Do you appear to have it all together, but in reality, are far from Him?

5. Consider the following verses and comment on how they reflect on how we are to live.

    Proverbs 11:1-4

    1 Peter 5:8

    1 John 3:8

6. Who did you feel was the most despicable of the dozen? Why?

7. Which of the people or sins did you most identify with?

PLEASE REVIEW

★ ★ ★ ★ ★

You have reached the awkward part of the book where I ask you to leave me a review on Amazon, Google, or Goodreads. Believe me, I hate this as much as you do. However, I am swallowing my pride and asking anyway. Please! Whether you loved or hated it, you have made it this far, so please leave a review. Here's the thing: reviews play a big role in determining whether or not someone will read my book. Leaving a review will help me out a lot. If you liked this study, please recommend it to others. Oh, and thanks for reading my book. It means the world to me.

The ~~Hold~~ Spirit   The Holy Spirit

I can't stand typos. If you are like me, you can't either. Typos are like gremlins. No matter how many times a book has been edited, they magically appear. So, if you see a typo I missed, please email me at timothyjmulder@gmail.com.

Thanks!

More by Timothy J. Mulder

Suffering in Silence: Ministering to Those With Mental Illness

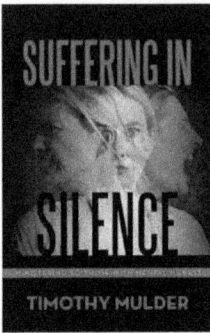

Mental illness affects millions of Americans. Often, those afflicted will develop substance abuse problems or will die from suicide. Surely, there must be something the church can do to help. The author considers questions such as: Why are those who suffer from mental illness so often misunderstood? What are common misconceptions about mental illness in the church? How are churches and other ministries well positioned to help people struggling with mental illness? How can you best minister to those with mental illness? Join the author as he explores how to better understand mental illness, so you may better minister to those who suffer from it.

Ruth: A Story of God's Redeeming Love

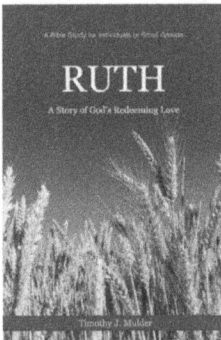

The Book of Ruth is one of the most famous short stories of all time. In just four chapters, the reader is exposed to faithlessness, death, unwavering integrity, and redemption. Ruth provides an intimate view into the back story of the lineage of King David. Set in the time of the Judges, when "everyone did what was right in their own eyes," the wholesomeness and honesty of Ruth are a welcome breath of fresh air. In this best-selling study, we cover such topics as God's loving-kindness, the foreshadowing of Christ, waiting on God's timing, the providence of God, and the redemption of Naomi. Join the author as he takes an in-depth, Reformed look into one of the greatest redemption stories of all time.

The Armchair Theologian's Guide to the Westminster Confession of Faith

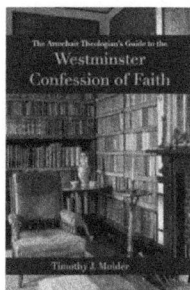

Do you ever feel as though you have read your Bible but wish you could better explain what you believe? Do you wonder how the Bible applies to our world today? Are you frustrated when confronted with viewpoints that are not Scriptural, but struggle to disprove them? The Westminster Confession of Faith is a topical arrangement of the Bible into doctrinal truths. It was written to organize the Bible into a unifying summary of what Christians believe and to combat heresy. The Westminster Confession of Faith is as relevant today as when it was written nearly 400 years ago. This book goes through the WCF in a user-friendly format, which includes the traditional and modern English versions of the WCF. It also highlights and counters unbiblical doctrine and creates talking points perfect for explaining Scripture to young believers or for cozy armchair discussions with friends.

What's Wrong With the Chosen?

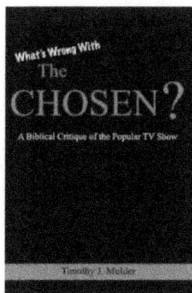

The Chosen is arguably the most well-received religious television series ever. It has received rave reviews, including a 9.8 out of 10 rating at IMDB. According to the show's producers, over 108 million people have watched since December 2022. It has been translated into over 50 languages and has multiple Bible studies based on its content. With such widespread support, what could be wrong with it? Is *The Chosen* Biblically accurate? Does it matter? A poll of reformed pastors and teachers showed that 87% are concerned about unbiblical content and consider the show a threat to uninformed believers. *What's Wrong With The Chosen?* provides a Biblical critique of the show. The author's four objections to *The Chosen* are discussed, followed by an in-depth analysis in which every scene in seasons 1-3 are evaluated for historical and Biblical accuracy.

www.ingramcontent.com/pod-product-compliance
Lightning Source LLC
LaVergne TN
LVHW091253080426
835510LV00007B/240